Hanging in There!

Hanging in There!

How to Resist Retirement from Life and Avoid Being Put Out to Pasture

by Peter Schwed

Illustrations by

Whitney Darrow, Jr.

Houghton Mifflin Company · Boston 1977

Library of Congress Cataloging in Publication Data

Schwed, Peter.
    Hanging in there!

    1. Retirement.   I. Title.
HQ1062.S36   301.43′5   77-7127
ISBN 0-395-25694-1

Printed in the United States of America
A 10 9 8 7 6 5 4 3 2 1

"The Proof" is reprinted from *Alexander King Presents Peter Altenberg's Evocations of Love;* copyright © 1960 by Simon and Schuster, Inc., by permission of Margie King.
The excerpts on pages 140–141 and 143 are from Notes and Comment in *The New Yorker.* Reprinted by permission; © 1976 by The New Yorker Magazine, Inc.
The cooperation of the staff of the American Association of Retired Persons is greatly appreciated.

For my dear wife, Antonia

Foreword

PETER SCHWED's *Hanging in There!* is obviously written by a person who is a realist but at the same time an optimist. That's my kind of guy. His sort of schizophrenic personality is probably explained by the fact (or in spite of it) that although he has been engaged in serious business all these years, he has an acute sense of humor. He doesn't ever let the content of his book or the ideas in it drag their feet. This goes well with the general mood, which is "up" all the way.

I truly believe that this is a needed book, not only for those who are growing older, but for the younger as well. It will help them realize that life is a system of constant beginnings rather than declines.

The author has said what needed to be said, and it boils down to this: "Old buddy, you're greater than you think you are in many more ways than you are aware of. You may not be getting any younger, but if 'the best is yet to come,' it will come only if invited."

Sam Levenson

Preface

THIS IS A BOOK about growing older, and what you can do about overcoming the very natural worries, frustrations, and hopelessness that affect so many people as they see themselves approaching, or past the "wrong side" of fifty. Both from observation and personal experience, I'm convinced that there is something you *can* do about reversing the gloom and feeling of helplessness that can so easily cripple one's future life at that stage, and the very first step — without which no further constructive program ever will take place — is to look at yourself objectively, evaluate circumstances realistically, change your priorities, choose a course of action, grit your teeth, and plunge into it.

There are certainly some situations in life where the old maxims extolling determination, self-discipline, and hard work can't achieve very much:

Setting a goal and sticking to it is not going to help you from going bald if baldness runs in your family.

Early to bed and early to rise won't enable you to take a place among the soloists in a choral group if you can't carry a tune.

Nothing will enable you to become king or queen of England if you're an American.

But there are many other objectives that *do* depend upon dogged resolve, both to get off the ground in the first place, and then to carry through:

You'll never go on a strict diet, or stick to it, without first determining that come hell or high water, you're going to do it.

The same is true of giving up smoking.

Then there is deciding to walk, rather than ride, to and from the office or the shopping center, when it's obvious you need more exercise.

Dogged resolve is the one characteristic you must summon up in order to succeed in hanging in there. Today ours is a society that has become increasingly worldly, and often cynical, about straightforward messages of inspiration. Ministers in the pulpit are likely to skirt around them; certainly it is not a tool for the psychiatrists, and even football coaches shy away from exhorting the boys to die for dear old Rutgers. I have grown up in a fairly sophisticated world and I know that there will be readers, some of them good friends, who will find this book simplistic, and wonder how any realist in the latter 1970s can believe so firmly in what seem to them to be naive and outdated platitudes. All I can answer is that I would not define optimism, risk-taking, and plain guts as being platitudes but rather as proven verities throughout history.

Contents

Part One

"We Shall Go On to the End . . .
We Shall Never Surrender."

Chapter One

Lock Your Desk and Throw the Key Away!

S OME FORTY YEARS AGO THE MOVIE DIRECTOR Leo Mc-
Carey made a really wonderful film which, on rare occasions if you're lucky, and have the stamina to stay up until
three or four in the morning, you can still see on television.
It was called *Make Way for Tomorrow*, and starred those
two great old character actors, Victor Moore and Beulah
Bondi. In his guide to *TV Movies* (Signet), Leonard Maltin's
review reads: "Sensitive film of elderly couple in financial
difficulty, shunted by their children, unwanted and unloved,
shatteringly true, beautifully done."

Admittedly the movie is a period piece in more ways than
one. It was made in the middle of the Great Depression of
the 1930s and so focused primarily upon the economic plight
of a family. But to the best of my knowledge, it introduced
the concept that was its title and that today, in a much more
youth-oriented society, has become an axiom in all walks of
life and particularly in business. A decade or two ago, realistic executives approaching their sixties would start thinking about the day when they'd either step down or be pushed
out and generously would begin to bring the best of the
thirty-five-year-olds into greater areas of authority and responsibility. Today, to an overwhelming extent, unless he is

3

the owner, a sixty-year-old man in business has already been told by his thirty-five to forty-five-year-old successor just when and how he's to call it a day, with the explanation that the firm has to make way for tomorrow. In fact, the groundwork may well have been laid even half a dozen years sooner, when our hero was in his early fifties and was innocently thinking he was in his business prime.

Let's face it. There are often good and solid reasons for this sort of thing to take place, apart from the very real possibility that the older man hasn't kept pace with changing times, and the younger man is better equipped to do a job. It's quite true that population growth has outstripped the rate of growth of the number of good jobs. Also widespread higher education has equipped more young people with qualifications and ambition, and if the old guys stay on forever, where and when will there be room for the comers? In any event, it's not the concern of this book to promulgate an opinion, pro or con, about the wisdom of these changing mores. It has happened, and you and I are not going to change it.

But here's the thing of it. Would we want to change matters if we could? Is it possible that now for the very first time in your entire life when you are neither pressed by obligations, nor appear to be needed very much any longer, you can see opportunities, set goals, achieve attainments that consciously or unconsciously you have always wanted to try, and never could?

My answer to that is a ringing YES, and I intend to prove it. In the vernacular of the sports world, this book is meant to be like a fight talk. (Knute Rockne, thou shouldst be living at this hour.) Phrases like "A team that won't be beaten can't be beaten" are out of fashion and considered corny today, but performances through the ages, in every aspect of living, are filled with examples of the underdog, the handicapped, the oppressed, rising to heights through sheer inspiration and drive.

Franklin D. Roosevelt spelled out the Four Freedoms as being freedom of speech, freedom of religion, freedom from want, and freedom from fear. Since that day the passion for another freedom — freedom to be oneself and "do your own thing" has taken its place among the major urges of the modern world. But this is often a very difficult thing for any conventionally brought up person to undertake, since it usually involves running counter to everything in one's heritage of conduct. Attractive as it may seem to you, a man who is a district sales manager, or to you, a woman who makes the daily routine run smoothly for her husband and three children in a suburban home, attractive as it may seem to cut loose and join a guru group in Big Sur, you are not likely to do it. There is too much social disapproval attached to it, even in your own mind. During those years when bringing home the bacon seemed the completely vital thing, both for yourself and others, doing anything else would appear to be a cop-out.

But eureka! Attain an age when society doesn't give a damn what you do, so long as you don't take too long getting out of sight and mind, and suddenly you're FREE! Free really for the very first time to try the things, or become the person that you may always have wanted for yourself. Up to now, if you are like most people, you have been blocked by the rules of your traditional upbringing. When you were young, the pressure was on you to do well in school and to be a credit to your parents. Later, new fetters bound you to the grindstone. Earn money, save for a rainy day, keep up the house, bear and raise good children. You may have loved your chains, or at least some of them, but you sure as the devil have never been free.

Now — suddenly — you are! It really doesn't matter how you came to be that way. Perhaps your company's procedure when an employee reached a certain birthday had its origins in the French Revolution, and your head simply rolled. You may have resented the guillotine, but you are finally free! Perhaps, whether you worked in an office or on a job, or even were self-employed, you awakened one day after years of not liking what you did very much and decided to lock your desk and throw the key away. In much the same vein as Christian Fletcher finally informed Captain Bligh how he felt about serving under him on the *Bounty,* you may have decided to walk out of a hateful or tiresome job run by an unpleasant employer. I'm not maintaining that everyone in such a position should, or even can follow such a course of action, but there are plenty who should, and don't. Perhaps you are one of them?

In any event, whether retirement is forced upon you or you choose it, you are now free! No one is likely to give a hoot about what you do, so long as you don't bother *them.* Your security may be gone, but so is the dread of risking it that shackled you in past years. So why not kick your heels in glee and start thinking of how you're going to enjoy the rest of your life? You haven't a thing to lose and, very possibly for the first time in your life, the world is your oyster.

Chapter Two

The Trouble with Pitching Horseshoes!

THIS IS AN ANTIRETIREMENT BOOK. I have no quarrel with the older man or woman who is looking forward to getting out of the rat race and assiduously studies every brochure or mail-order advertisement about the glories of "senior communities." Calculated retirement living may well be the right answer for many people who feel that the ideal way for them to pass the "golden years" is to settle in a warm climate, gossip with neighbors of their own age while sitting on a porch playing cards or knitting, and perhaps play a few holes of golf using a golf cart. Or pitch horseshoes. Or bake a cake.

Really severe physical infirmities can be a good reason for selecting such a way of life. Simple weariness or lack of future ambition can be another (but if it's this last be sure that the lack of ambition isn't merely lack of ideas, or of confidence in yourself). But do be aware that if and when you choose to pass your latter years in this fashion, the applicable verb is certainly "pass." Brother — sister — you will have given up on *living* in those years!

Not for me! Not for you either if the title of this book, and what you have read so far, intrigues you. Let me tell you how I happen to be writing it.

Something over a dozen years ago, our children having grown past the nursing and feeding age, and I being heavily involved in my job, my dear wife looked over a YWCA catalogue one day and decided to take a course. Among her many other attractions and attainments, she is an imaginative sketcher and extremely adept with her hands. So she chose to study and learn enameling, which is the creation of artistic objects such as jewelry, sculpture, wall hangings, bowls, and so forth, by fusing enamels (colored powdered glass) to the surface of a metal (such as copper or silver). She proved to be very good at it from the very beginning, and loved doing it so much that she bought a kiln, which was installed in a spot in our apartment where it was least likely to get in the way, or incinerate our children or our cat. Beautiful one-of-a-kind pieces started appearing all over the house and, while my wife kept most of them and our daughters absconded with some, a number of others were displayed in group shows and in art galleries. Some time later, the sponsors of her enamels course at the Y, the Craft Students League, asked Toni to become the teacher of a course of her own and, for the past half dozen years, she has been doing that as well as continuing with her own enameling.

Meanwhile, back at the office where, at the time when Toni first took up enameling, I had been the administrative boss (but never an owner — just a salaried employee), the first rumblings of make way for tomorrow were just beginning to be felt by me. Nothing so tangible as a change in status, to say nothing of a fear of losing my job, was threatened, but two new (and then quite upsetting) concepts were more or less insidiously floated across my consciousness. The first was that, within short years, a new and vital administration ought to take over so that the firm's long-term future could be assured. The second was that the one-man owner, himself a few years older than I, was likely to accept one or the other of the offers that came to him from time to time from conglomerates eager to acquire his company. That almost surely would mean a number of new brooms at work sweeping clean.

The fact is that both of these apparently dire possibilities have indeed taken place since then, but in retrospect I find I'm thankful that it all happened when and as it did. I'm still happily on the job with less responsibility and work (more of this in Chapter 6, which deals with how best to conduct yourself if and when this happens to you), and I did get enough advance warning of what was going to take place to prepare my mind and ideas about the best way to face up to it.

The event that really did for me what I'd hope this book might do for you took place three or four years ago. One evening Toni gingerly removed a champlevé pendant from her kiln, hovered over it watching the colors change as the piece started to cool, and said: "You know, I think I'm set for life. I simply love doing this, and it occupies my time and imagination whenever there's nothing else on tap that I have to do or want to do. You can leave me sketching a design in the morning as you go off to your office, and I can get so intent upon working out the piece that I keep at it all day, and you have to tear me away from it when you come home. With a little bit of luck and my enameling, I don't think I'm ever going to have to wonder what to do with my time."

I grunted and said "Damn it!" as I saw Walt Frazier of the Knicks miss a jump shot from the key in the televised playoff basketball game I was watching. Toni was not to be diverted.

"You ought to get onto something comparable yourself, Peter. I can sense from what I know that you think the day could very well come, perhaps sooner than you once thought, when you'll either want to retire or be pushed into it. What do you figure on doing then? I know you're mad about reading, and playing tennis, but they're not enough, and God knows that watching television isn't. You'll need something to do with your mind, or your hands, and preferably with both."

Frazier made his next shot, and the beer commercial was now prattling away during a time-out. I had a chance to reply.

"Well, darling, that thought has indeed vaguely crossed my mind, and my idea was that if and when the day came, I'd pull out my typewriter, stick a piece of paper in it, and stare at it. I know I rather enjoy writing, and I've been writing jacket copy and publicity releases for books for years as part of my job. Some of it's been pretty good — I have a facility for stringing one word after another without too much anguish. But I do have one rather serious problem."

"What's that, dear?"

"I haven't anything to say."

That was the moment when *I* received the fight talk that I needed. I won't try to recapture her exact words, but Toni insisted that if I just thought about it all, and actually tried to write something out of my own knowledge or imagination, the typewriter keys would soon start clicking away. And the time to start doing it was not when I actually was facing retirement, and perhaps in some despair about it, but *now*. That way, when the time came, I might be as much in the groove, about knowing what to do with all that spare time, as she already was.

My Antonia is a knowing, smart lady, and when she talks seriously to me, I listen. So within a week I sat down and wrote a humorous article about how publishers think up titles for books, and it was published. I wrote two articles about tennis, and each of them was taken by a magazine. That led a book publisher to ask me to write a short tennis book to be part of a series they were putting out, and I did that so quickly and satisfactorily that they asked me to do a second book. I wrote a sentimental reminiscence of an episode that took place in England when I was a soldier there in World War II for a year prior to D-Day, and *that* was bought by a magazine too. Finally (at least up to now), I wrote a real, full-length book about my first job during the Depression — a combination of social history, personal anecdotes, and humor — that was accepted by still another book publisher, and which was received so well by the book critics that, if sales hadn't been on the comparatively modest side, it would have swollen my hat size out of recognition.

But whether I ever make real money out of my writing or not isn't the point. "Hanging in there" is not meant to imply that you have to be a flaming success at whatever you decide to undertake, or even that you make any money at all. Between Social Security and pensions, most of us who have worked a number of years are not actually going to have to starve or sleep on park benches in our old age. We may have to tighten our belts and even live on a very different scale, but we're likely to get by. What is more, up to age seventy-two, the more extra money a retiree makes, the less Social Security he or she gets paid so, like many paradoxical things in life, they've got you coming and going.

No. The idea is to pick out a new occupation for yourself that will intrigue and interest you and afford you satisfaction. While mind reading is not one of my own occupations or accomplishments, I can guess what you may be thinking, and it could quite understandably go something like this:

"That's all well and good for you to say, but how can a person have any realistic confidence that he or she is going to be *able* to do what may intrigue or interest him or her? Your wife took up enameling, but she obviously had some basic artistic skills. You decided to try writing, but facility with words and writing had always been part of your background and work. I know you would also have been 'intrigued and interested' in becoming the next Olympic decathlon champion but, leaving aside the fact that you're in your sixties, do you think you'd be likely to get very far toward that ambition? All right — I'm kidding — but suppose you, who come from a family of tin ears and who never has had any real musical training or taste, decided you now wanted to see if you could play an instrument? Or even compose? Wouldn't that be just about as impractical an idea as the decathlon one?"

A good question, but the answer is no — it wouldn't. Don't turn off the light quite yet: I'm taking up the question in the next chapter.

Chapter Three

99 *Percent Perspiration*

I T WOULD BE DIFFICULT to pick many people in history
whose accomplishments seem to indicate the sort of mind
and abilities that almost no one can match better than
Thomas Alva Edison. Yet it was Edison himself who maintained stoutly that he was not being gracefully over-modest
when he declaimed that genius was 99 percent perspiration
and 1 percent inspiration.

He may have been exaggerating the percentage break-
down for the sake of effect, but I'm convinced that his basic
point is valid. People are capable of learning and doing
almost everything that isn't obviously beyond their physical
capabilities. (There go my decathlon ambitions. Oh, well.)
Everyone knows his own story best, and the opinions he
picks up throughout life are the soundest when they are
formed as the result of personal experience. So again, but
only because it's my own most convincing way to try to
prove Edison was right, I'm going to tell you what once happened to me.

At the very beginning of 1942, shortly after Pearl Harbor,
I received "Greetings!" from the president, and went into
the army. As a draftee I had no choice of service or specialty, and was sent wherever chance ordained which, in my
case, turned out to be field artillery. Now those of you
whose hobbies haven't included field artillery — as mine cer-

tainly hadn't — may think that it consists of putting a big bullet (the word is "projectile") into a big gun (the howitzer) and pulling a string (lanyard). You are absolutely right insofar as that goes, but there are quite a few more things involved in getting this done effectively, and a good field artilleryman has to learn all of them to some extent. He has to learn the specialty to which he's assigned very thoroughly.

An urban type like myself, and particularly one who had a pretty fair degree of mathematical aptitude, didn't find most of these things too intimidating to learn. The first, the science of *Gunnery*, is something that anyone with a flair for mathematics actually would find fun, if it didn't involve warfare and killing. So that was no sweat, nor was *Survey*, involving meticulous work with transits and surveyors' chains and, once again, mathematics. *Motors*, where you were supposed to pick up enough knowledge to be able to have a reasonable stab at fixing small mechanical problems that might arise in a jeep or a truck, began to get me into deeper waters. I had driven cars since I was sixteen, but I had never changed a sparkplug. Still, I could handle a short course in motors without flinching. The same was true of that comparatively dull course to me, *tactics*, which I obviously wasn't ever going to have to use in a practical sense. I wasn't going to rise high enough and fast enough to be in a position where anyone was going to ask me how to run a war.

With *Communications*, however, we come to the area of my army experience that really makes the point I'm trying to prove. Here's a quick rundown on what's involved in artillery communications.

Observers have to communicate back and forth with the fire direction center, or direct with a gun crew. If it's possible, this is done via field telephones: if it isn't, it's accomplished by radio. A telephone set-up involves reconnaissance to determine where and how telephone wire can be laid and strung, and then you've got to go out and do it. Miles of wire, splices, overhead crossings and ties, terminal connections, a command post switchboard and its operation, the knowledge of how to strip and repair a field telephone. And I forget what else, but you get the idea. Radio communication involves less work, but learning something about the innards and fine tuning of a radio is much more complicated than the equivalents of a telephone, and there's more than one type of radio used, each quite different from the other.

Now I grew up in a completely nonmechanical family, where no one ever even considered trying to fix a leaky water

tap by inserting a new washer. The plumber did that. If the lights in the house suddenly went out, we didn't make for the fuse box for a couple of very good reasons. We didn't know where it was and, if we did, would have had no notion what to do. We called an electrician. Not a mechanical family, as I've said. So when all this communications stuff loomed across my punch-drunk horizon I thought, and continued to think throughout the early days of training in it, that if anyone was going to depend upon me to perform even adequately at this sort of thing, Germany was going to win the war.

Do you know what happened? I not only got to like it, but I got good enough at it all to become the communications officer of our outfit. You could have knocked me over with a transistor.

Then I also had to learn to transmit and receive Morse code messages at fairly high speeds. That required skills of ear and touch that I certainly wouldn't think I had an aptitude for, but it turned out that it was one of my better specialties. In fact, if worse ever comes to worst, and if Western Union is still around with quiet little offices in nice little towns where the telegrapher can read plenty of books while waiting for the next buzz of the *dit-dah*, I may know where to turn for a retirement job.

Are you thinking that all this may indeed have been possible and an eye-opener for me, but how about the next fellow who may not have had as good educational advantages as I? Was he able to learn and enjoy new skills too?

You bet.

I can cite you men in our outfit who never went past a grade school education who became wizards at some of the things I've described. Because we were forced to try our hands at all sorts of matters we knew nothing of, the curious and eager among us got interested and became good at them. That convinces me, even more, that if one were not forced into something, but rather selected it as a potentially fascinating thing to do, it would be mastered.

So if you have been a white-collar desk worker all your adult life, it's quite possible that your way of hanging in there in later years might well be to study machines or carpentry, and set up your own workshop, whether it turns out to be purely for fun or possibly for profit as well. A retired policeman might want to see what he can do with oil painting. Not everyone can make such a spectacular and successful change as Paul Gauguin did after more than a dozen years in a bank, or Grandma Moses after decades of being a conventional housewife, but success and recognition are not the real points: accomplishment and self-satisfaction and enjoyment are.

A Few Questions for You to Think About

This, and the other questions that will appear later, are not tests in the traditional sense, in that no one is going to give you a grade on them, or even a "pass" or "fail" notation. Instead they are simply sets of questions, with alternative answers, that may help you see more clearly not only the sort of person you are, but the person you potentially might be.

The reason these tests are not of a more definitive sort, in which you come up with a numerical result that indicates your best potential as you grow older is to be another Albert Einstein or a night watchman, is that such a test, even if I were qualified to devise one (which I'm not), would be both impracticable and meaningless.

There are far too many variables among the people who might be intrigued or inspired by the messages in this book. You can be a traditionally well-educated elderly person who stopped being intellectually curious the day you left school or college. You can be full of ambition, drive, and ideas, but now find yourself with no financial resources at all with which to undertake a new life, since your income from now on appears to be barely more than that required for sustenance. You can be as healthy as you were in your youth, or you may be crippled by arthritis. Any attempt to correlate so diverse a group of factors into a grade that would embody them all, and give you an idea of how good a candidate you are for successfully hanging in there, would be a bootless undertaking.

So I am just posing some questions here for you to think about, as they may apply to yourself. Alternative answers to each are also given, but you could well have different ones than any I propose as possibilities. Finally, after each question, you'll find a summation of what I think the various answers convey about you with respect to the topic of this book.

1. How old are you?

_____ Under 35
_____ 35–45
_____ 45–55
_____ 55–65
_____ 65 or older

If you are under thirty-five, give the book to your parents. You yourself may find it of value a decade or two from now: I hope it will still be in print.

If you are thirty-five–forty-five, the chances are that you'll feel the book doesn't yet have much significance for you. That is probably true, but don't be too sure. As the years go by, the pressures for even earlier retirement ages are coming from all directions. A good example is the case of former Lieutenant Colonel Bob Murgia, who was forced to retire as head of the Massachusetts State Police on the grounds of age, although he was only fifty years old and admittedly physically vigorous, athletic, and so fully in command of his mental and administrative capacities that his case became an issue for the Supreme Court.

Disappointingly, the Court ruled 7 to 1 that it was legal for the Massachusetts government to dismiss Colonel Murgia, but in his eloquent dissent Justice Thurgood Marshall pointed out that the Court's decision in this particular case — dealing with a specific professional group subject to unusual demands for physical stamina — "does not imply that

must face up to things right now is because, at the very best, attitudes of the world toward you are going to change as you approach, and as you slide into, senior citizenship. Life is not going to be the same for you as it has been, and it's up to you — and only you — to try to see to it that the change will not turn out to be shattering, and a catastrophe, but very possibly a rebirth of excitement and a blessing.

If you are sixty-five or over, the same philosophy applies. You might have been better off and further along the road to a gratifying old age if you had set out to experiment with new ideas and goals some years earlier, but there are countless examples, a few of which are cited later in this book, that prove that it's never too late to start.

2. Which sex are you?

_____ Man
_____ Woman

This is an unimportant question, and I've only put it in to be able to say that, as far as the significance of this book is concerned, things are equally applicable to men and to women. There are some special aspects that pertain to women who have always been homemakers, however, and they are the basis of Chapter 7.

3. Is there a specific thing you perhaps always wanted to do, but which you never attempted? If yes, why didn't you?

_____ Too tied down to the treadmill.
_____ Insufficient money.
_____ Thought it beyond my capabilities.
_____ Simply never got around to it.

If no, how do you explain that to yourself?

_____ Nothing interested me.

_____ No confidence that I could do anything more than the simple work I had always performed.

Let's look first at the possible explanation offered if your reply was yes. Two of them, the first and the last, can now be disregarded. You are not going to be tied down any more, and you now have nothing but plenty of time in which to get around to doing what you might dearly have wanted to do for a long time. That leaves the other two explanations: not enough money and fear that you were not up to achieving what you'd like to do.

Money. I am presuming that your ambitions at this stage of life are not so grandiose as to be hopelessly out of grasp as far as financing is concerned. You are not thinking of designing and building a new 12-meter yacht to enter the next competition for the America's Cup, are you? You're not wistfully contemplating erecting a fashionable resort on a Caribbean island? Good.

More likely, you wish to be doing something that you'd enjoy and that might produce some money, and that would essentially be a satisfying way of life for you. There are two avenues existing: You may be lucky enough to find a new job that fits these aims (particularly if you're not afraid of tackling something you've never done before), or you can strike out on your own.

This latter may or may not require that you have some original capital of your own at the outset.

Well, I imagine you've noticed that since we were young an elaborate and very expansive credit society has sprung up. It is really quite practical these days for people to obtain loans, from private banking sources to governmental and state agencies, to enable them to embark upon small business undertakings. If your past record and character appear to be reasonably good, you're not going to need anything too unattainable in the way of collateral or cosigners to float the sort of small loan you probably require. (If this isn't true let's *never* believe a television commercial about your friendly banker again!)

So that leaves nothing standing in your way except your fear that, despite your attraction toward trying a new enterprise, you may not have the capability to carry it off. Well, the greater part of Chapter 2 was devoted to my trying to explode this myth. If you've never been exposed to something, you have no way of knowing whether you indeed will be a dodo at it or, perhaps, an absolute wizard. The truth is likely to be in between, but my experience tells me strongly that it's more likely to be closer to the second than the first. Simple competence at almost all things is within our reach if we care enough to try.

All right. Let's say you either have the capital you require, or can raise it. The warning here is to be sure that you have enough not only to get started, but to keep going for a few months, for almost invariably it takes a little while before the returns on even a fairly successful little business can really be chalked up in the black ink column. And all right, again. You are confident that you do have the native good business sense and the interest and ability to carry out the enterprise you choose for yourself. Watch out for one more thing, before you take such a plunge! Is there a real *need* in your community for that particular enterprise?

For many summers I've lived in a small Connecticut town. The shopping area is all of three or four blocks long, but we have two dentists, two barbers, two pharmacies, two marinas, two liquor stores, and five real estate agents! I don't know how each of them is faring, but I do know that if I were to try to hang out my shingle in that town I would not choose to be a dentist, a barber, a druggist, a small-boatyard operator, a liquor dealer, or a real estate agent. There is one hardware shop, a delicatessen, a market, a dress shop, a beauty shop, a restaurant (expensive), and, except for the post office and the fire house, that's about it. Maybe there's room for competition in some of those areas, but if I were retiring to that town, and wanted to start up a small business of my own, I'd establish a place where young people could come and sit down and enjoy each other's company at a table over a modestly priced sandwich and coffee, or ice cream, or a glass of soda pop, or beer if the law permitted. That would be filling a need in this particular small town, and I suspect that anyone who had the inclination to tackle it, and had sufficient capital to get it started and going for a while, would make a success of it.

And now, sadly, we have to consider what to do about you if your reply was no, and your explanations of why you never wanted to try anything were as defeatist as you indicated. There isn't much to say, and it may be too late for the leopard to change its spots. But change them you should and must, if the rest of your life is not going to be the same, and even worse, than the apparently dreary one you've endured up to now. Perhaps you actually are as spiritless and as much of a dullard as your reply makes you out to be, but I don't believe it for one very good reason. You not only can read a book but you are reading this particular book right now. That indicates you *must* want to live a more productive life in the future, and the wanting is half the battle. And here's the thrilling part of it for you in particular. If you can actually reach out for new goals, with the handicap your past has laden you with, yours will be the greatest triumph and satisfaction of all.

Part Two

The View from the Other Side of the Hill

Chapter Four

Vive la Différence!

Q UICKLY — BEFORE YOU ACCUSE ME of trapping you into being curious about this chapter because its title indicates that it may be a companion work to *The Joy of Sex* — it isn't. Sex is going to get some mention later in this book when perhaps you least expect it, but not right now.

The fact is that "la différence," in the sense that I'm about to suggest to you, is the fundamental message behind every other idea or philosophy that arises in these pages. This is what I mean by it. When you are faced with a change in life-style because of advancing years, you can either be resigned to it or accept it, and your choice will spell as enormous a difference in your subsequent well-being as there is in the bare dictionary definitions of these two words that, at first glance, seem to mean somewhat the same thing. Let's look at what the dictionary says:

Resignation means "a submissive attitude or state, unresisting acquiescence." Its synonyms are meekness, patience, and compliance. If you intend to hang in there, resignation is for the birds!

Acceptance means "the act of taking or receiving something offered, favorable reception." Its synonyms are approval and favor. If you intend to hang in there, realistic and constructive acceptance of your situation can lead to your becoming a better and happier man or woman than you ever were.

Vive la différence between resignation and acceptance!

The fact is that being able to make this distinction and, more important, to act in the spirit of acceptance rather than resignation, isn't at all confined to senior citizen problems. Throughout life everyone encounters setbacks, bad luck, and tragedies. Those who summon up the unquenchable human spirit that I believe exists in all us, accepting reverses and then acting courageously rather than merely being resigned to misfortune, are the ones who have a chance for new accomplishments and success. At the very least, they achieve personal fulfillment in influencing their own destinies. In the inbetween cases, the small businessman wiped out by unfortunate factors, not of his making, makes a comeback and re-establishes himself. At the summit, history produces many giants who accepted and *did* things about adversity, even with apparently hopeless physical handicaps. Think of the brilliant and inspiring career that Helen Keller carved out throughout her life, despite being both deaf and blind from earliest infancy!

Gearing your mind to the idea that your life is going to change in some respects in your latter years should be no more frightening than many comparable changes you had to make, or chose to make, in the past. How about the first time you ever left home to go away to school or camp? Were you frightened as you walked into your first job? How severe were your qualms about how you'd survive the entirely new sort of life that getting married involves? Having children? Moving to a new locality? Certainly you've faced some or all of these potentially violent upheavals of a previous existence, and whether they turned out for better or for worse, surely the way to go forward to meet them was with the spirit of acceptance, rather than of resignation. The one not only can, but is likely to meet with success: the other is foredoomed.

Let's face it. The only reason why you who have been courageous and optimistic throughout earlier years now face any change in circumstances with fear and despair may well be because you have suffered hardening of the mind and spirit. You are the same person you always were, with the same mind and interests and capacity for emotions. You may have lost something physically — how much, and how important it may or may not be, and what you can do about it is discussed in Chapter 8 — but this forty-five or fifty-five or sixty-five-year-old specimen we have here under the microscope is *you!* The same you who has successfully negotiated life up to this point without being run over by a truck or settling down in a rest home as the result of incurring a case of tennis elbow or housemaid's knee. Admittedly, some part of the traumatic dread people have about retirement, or the threat of it, is connected to the thought that one has passed the crest of life's hill and is starting down the other side of it. That's a logical and natural enough thought to make anyone gloomy on occasion — for as long as fifteen seconds at a time. But that's just about the length of time it's worth. You could have been Keats and have died at the age of twenty-six; but now that you have survived to the age you are, you're not at all an impossible candidate to live as long as the two Pablos, Picasso and Casals, both of whom were continuing to exercise their marvelous gifts most successfully when they were ninety, to say nothing of the many others whose inspiring latter years' achievements you'll encounter in Chapter 9.

The life insurance actuaries tell us that these days, if one lives to the age a reader of this book is likely to be, a man's expectancy is no longer merely threescore and ten, but somewhat into his eighties; a woman's, well into hers. Think about that. Are you really content to be "resigned" to whatever lies in store for you for, let us say, *twenty years?*

No. A thousand times — no. People don't wear out as much as they rust out. You must find a project and set goals for yourself. Alexander Dumas's Count of Monte Cristo had his: He spent twenty years digging his way out of the prison of the Chateau d'If with a teaspoon. He had something to do every day! When he succeeded he cried out "The world is mine!" Perhaps you may not wish to emulate the count literally, but you really have nothing to lose and everything to gain if you decide to tackle *anything* that intrigues you. You are in a position to dare more than you ever have risked in the past. When you were climbing up one side of the hill,

your life and occupations were circumscribed, at least to a large extent, by what you, your dependents, and society expected of you. The only view in sight really was the top of the hill.

Here, cresting the peak and looking down on the other side, the view can be infinitely more expansive and beautifully exciting.

Chapter Five

Your Inner Self

S HAKESPEARE PUT TOO SPECIFIC a goal on Malvolio's
sphere of vision in *Twelfth Night,* when he had him de-
claim that some are born great, some achieve greatness, and
some have greatness thrust upon them. Most of us are not
too concerned about greatness, but everybody is concerned
with the course his or her life takes and the jobs we face in
it, and Malvolio's three alternatives may well apply.

The children of the very wealthy, and those of the desperately poor, have a strong chance of being born to what
they'll be undertaking. The ambitious, single-minded person
with a very tangible goal may achieve the career that is his
target. But on the whole, the majority of people rather wander into adulthood without any real idea of what their life's
work is going to be, and they eventually have it thrust upon
them.

The most fortunate of them come to love it. The great
middle sector accepts and tolerates it, alternately liking and
disliking what they do in the working hours. The really unfortunate may be chained to an existence they despise. Yet
regardless of what fate or luck holds in store for them, there
is a host of middle-aged or elderly people who have either
been forced, or have chosen, to suppress their inner urges to
try something else. Perhaps they have wished for an entirely
different career, and were either unable or unadventurous

enough to dare it. Perhaps they were quite content with their way of life, although they did have enthusiasms that would have enlarged their horizons and pleasure, but that they never got around to undertake even as a hobby. It's hard to step off a treadmill, particularly if your bread and butter depends upon it.

Then the time arrives about which this book is concerned. Your life is going to change to some considerable extent, for no reason except that you're getting older and the make-way-for-tomorrow syndrome has caught up with you. Perhaps it's still years away, and you are only getting signals that it's impending for the first time now. Perhaps it descends upon you with a crash, and you're asked to clear out your desk by next Monday. Obviously the latter is a lot more traumatic, but if you are in the position to have to accept the fact that such callousness is likely in advance of when it takes place (if it does), you can start rolling up your sleeves and gearing your spirit and mind to a new — and very possibly better life — just as effectively as if you were going to be eased out more gracefully.

Here is the moment to listen to what your inner self may have been trying to tell you for decades. All that time daily, from the ringing of the alarm clock in the morning to the closing whistle, you've been working at something you *had* to do. It has been something like having to pump hard at the pedals of a bicycle to climb a steep slope. Maybe it's been nothing but hard work for you, whether you were in a machine shop, an office, or at home with the housework and the care of the children. Conversely, maybe you enjoyed every minute of it — after all, pumping a bike is good exercise out in the open air. But don't tell me that it isn't a relief to reach the top of the slope and see level ground ahead, where you can pedal easily, or even spot a gradual descent down which you can actually *coast!* That's a time for real enjoyment, and doing what's fun on a bicycle. You may even want to release the handlebars and sing out to the world, "Look! No hands!"

A comparable exhilaration, when you see yourself on the way toward getting off your treadmill, is to search out the interests you've kept dormant within your inner self for one reason or another, and start *doing* them. The reason catalogues for correspondence schools are so bulky is because there are so very many things in the world that can be undertaken. Perhaps you feel that yes, you have always had a sneaking urge to learn how to play a musical instrument, to be a real estate agent, to repair mechanical objects, to paint in oils, to be a weather forecaster, or to assist people prepare their income-tax forms. (I know there must be some who do that, because advertisements and the yellow pages of the telephone directory say so. There are also people who choose the circus career of being shot out of cannons.) The point is, no matter what your inner self reveals to you as your unfulfilled urge, now is the time to have a stab at it. Maybe you'll have no real talent for it, but the army experience I recounted earlier made me confident that we simply don't know what we can do until we try. Let's say that you always felt it would be fun to be a librarian but, given the opportunity, find it is uninspiring and dull. You'll still have time to unearth another submerged yen in your inner self that will work out more satisfyingly for you, perhaps being involved in an agency for the rehabilitation of drug addicts or working on ships in a marina.

Who knows what may be right for you? Probably not even you yourself until you've given it a whirl. The point is that now you are consciously choosing something that appeals to you as being either rewarding or fun, ideally both, but when I say "rewarding" I primarily mean rewarding in spirit. If you can make money in this, your second life, that's wonderful, but if you can't you're no worse off in that respect than if you just give up in the latter years of your life and do nothing. No one gets paid for doing nothing — or at least that's the theory.

Up to now, the message in this book has been confined to trying to get you to think constructively, and not at all despairingly, about its topic. The aperitif and the appetizer have been served, but we haven't gotten down to the meat and potatoes. After all, one reader may be in any of a number of circumstances quite different from another, and while generalities may be encouraging or even inspiring, it's time for some particulars.   Perhaps you're still on the job and intend to continue to be so for some time to come, currently only seeing smoke signals on the horizon that tell you that life will not go on the same way for you forever. Maybe you actually are either about to bow out, or already have. And then, again, you may never have had a conventional job at all, but have much the same dreads and uncertainties coming at you as if you had — I am thinking particularly of the mature woman whose fundamental role as housewife and mother no longer appears so vital. All are likely to have comparable worries — worries that can best be worked out by adopting new frames of mind. Each will probably come up with a different one, but the goal will be the same. The new priority can produce great enjoyment and opportunity for the person whose life-style is changing, so now let's start examining particular special problems and prospects.

Chapter Six

Plenty of Room in the Rear of the Bus!

L ET'S LOOK FIRST at the working man or woman who, between being good at the job and having an enlightened or paternalistic employer, is *not* going to be turned out onto the streets at any specific retirement age. As long as that employee never did get too far up the ladder of position and power in an organization, but simply was an efficient salaried person performing a function, all will probably go on just as it always did, with separation from the office only taking place at a time that's mutually agreeable. Probably no problem will exist unless the old retainer starts threatening the *Guinness Book of World Records* for longevity — there does come a point when even the most generous and understanding of employers has to point out kindly that the business would be a little better off with someone who didn't fall asleep at his desk for an hour every morning and every afternoon. In business, there certainly is such a thing as outstaying your welcome, but that is not what this chapter is about.

What if you are a person who has had a long and relatively successful working career and, as a result, in the period of mid-life to senior years, has attained a real measure of authority and status? Then suddenly you become aware that the make-way-for-tomorrow syndrome is sending up smoke signals that say that within a few years (or months or weeks or days depending upon how one's executioners decide to let the ax fall), some younger genius is going to take over your department (or, if you're a bigger boss, your entire division, or your job of administering a company, or your seat on the board of directors). You're not going to be fired, you understand, but the firm has to look ahead to the next quarter of a century, so it makes sense that someone who seems likely to stay the course takes over.

Once again, I am not criticizing the logic or the necessity for a business organization to come to such a conclusion and to act upon it. I'm reasonably sure that it's more often justified than not, but that discussion — pro and con — belongs to a book on corporate personnel. At this point, we, and this particular book, are concerned about the individual to whom such a dictum is given, and what he or she can best do about it.

It takes a more pragmatic person than almost any of us are to accept an experience like this without, at the least, initially feeling wounded and, at the worst, feeling almost suicidal. Obviously it isn't as traumatic as being forcibly thrown out, but it's often a staggering blow to one's pride and to one's contentment with life, both in the present and the future. Yet, in most cases, a person does decide to accept it and to live with it, and does so for any number of reasons. You may need the job and the money that goes with it, and finding another comparable one may well be virtually impossible at your age. You may like your work very much, or certainly more than any other for which you feel equipped, and not want either to change or to toss in the towel in a fit of resentment. You may be very attached to the people with whom you work (with the probable exception of the person who delivered the blow), and would miss not being with them. Finally, you may think that they'll find out what a mistake they're making one of these days, and ask you to run things again. (Don't bet on this last, no matter how good you think you are. Even if you actually are that good. If there's one aspect of business that is axiomatic, it is that no one is indispensable.)

No. Lick your wounds as quickly as you can and face up to the very real truth that sulking will get you nowhere except further down a path of self-pity, but, instead, there are now open roads ahead for you that can be gratifyingly constructive, satisfying, and enjoyable.

If you were to find yourself in this position, there is a first giant mental step you *must* take. Once you have taken it, everything that follows can be for the good. That first step is this book's Golden Rule, and applies with equal force to every variation of hanging in there that I write about, whether you are a man or a woman, whether you are still working on the old job past retirement age, or tossed out on your ear, whether you are continuing to live where you always have or have picked up stakes and gone elsewhere, whether you're in splendid health or not. It could well be the alternative title to this book, and it's so important that it is set off here — and will occasionally continue to be throughout the rest of the book — in capital letters within a box. It is:

> CHANGE YOUR PRIORITIES!

The executive who is going to continue to work for his old firm, but with his functions curtailed, has considerably less to alter in the way of priorities than those, whom we shall meet, who truly will have to undergo a deep sea change.

They not only are faced with the necessity for a new mental approach, but may well be learning completely new physical skills and occupations, whereas our executive merely has to come to terms with himself philosophically about the new, and very possibly pleasanter, role he will be playing. Once he accepts the idea that what is happening is not of his making, that he can't be faulted for the fact that he's older and his company is not villainous but is logically trying to assure its future by bringing in youth, he can shrug his shoulders and realize that's the way the corporate cookie crumbles. There's no reason for either petulance or resentment. At this stage, he is ready to start thinking constructively about what his future conduct and priorities should be, if he's going to continue to be happy and effective.

Here is the truth of it in a situation like this. It's a reasonable assumption that you've been a good and effective worker, respected and pleasant enough to have around, if they've told you that they'd be glad to have you stay on up to, or even well past normal retirement age. They value you and your work, and will continue to do so. No one thinks you have lost your marbles, or are no longer playing with a full deck. You have valuable knowledge and experience, perhaps more than anyone else. You can certainly continue to contribute, and earn your salt.

So, if that's the case, why is this happening? It's simply because you can't be counted upon to last forever, and an enterprising firm should conduct its affairs as if the firm will last forever. In such a company it's the leaders, from the top boss down through the department heads, whose excellence or lack of it spells success or disaster. The firm has to develop those leaders and put them in the seats of control early enough to effect smooth transitions. It wouldn't be very wise if an important position had to be filled from a grab bag the day after its former occupant passed from the scene for one reason or the other. That is the primary, and often the only, reason why good people begin to be elbowed aside while still in their fifties and almost invariably after sixty.

But hear this. Your successors don't hate you. They are not angry with you, nor do they wish you ill. If they are smart enough to take your place, they are smart enough to know that one of these days, perhaps as little as ten but almost surely fifteen or twenty years from now, they will be in the same position themselves. Someone will be whispering or shouting in *their* ears, "Make way for tomorrow!" They don't want to set a precedent that may boomerang on them some day.

No. Since you're good and still productive, the only things they need to take from you are the power and authority you've been accustomed to enjoy. Your first new priority, then, is a negative one. Give up power and authority gracefully. As you then pick up new, positive priorities, you may well find in retrospect that you are glad about the change taking place when it did. It's quite possible that you never did "enjoy" wielding power and authority, unless you were endowed with a high quota of sadism at birth, but you only really enjoyed the money and attention it brought you.

When you give up power and authority, you also give up the headaches, the pressures, and the ulcers that so frequently go with it. You will find that when you slip into the new scheme of things with a forward-looking and constructive spirit, you may be happier than you've been for years. Continue to do what you can do well, but let someone else steer the ship from now on. You've had that, it's in the record book (and you always were a little nervous about the rocky reefs anyhow). Let George do it now; let George be the skipper. When George sees that you're not overtly hostile (as so many people who find themselves in this position are, and that is completely self-destructive), nor are you even resentful, he is most likely to leave you alone in every other respect. No one wants unnecessarily to shame or denigrate elderly associates; they simply don't want them giving orders any more. It's someone else's turn. So things like your office and your secretary are not likely to be taken away, nor your benefits and perquisites. You may work just as hard as ever, but now that the burden of responsibility is off your shoulders, it's up to you to decide whether you care to do so or not. Is that so bad? You always did want to linger a little longer over lunch, or take off somewhat earlier on Friday afternoons for the weekend, and now you can do so without any guilt feelings about missing something Important.

More significantly, you can now grasp the opportunity to enlarge horizons that up to now had been limited by the requirements of a constant 9-to-5 attention to every detail and supervision of a job. Volunteer to serve on committees of your industry's association. Make speeches or teach at an adult education course in your field, if that is something you might be good at. Be *visible* in all the areas that the new young geniuses probably think of as eyewash, since none of it is too likely to be allied to the direct prosperity of your firm. That way you will relieve your successor, who is breaking his skull over such exciting matters as escalating costs, inventory control, and sales resistance, from having to deal with such quiet, thoughtful, time-consuming matters as committee meetings of the industry.

Much of what you'll now do is indeed likely to be eyewash, but it's a decidedly pleasant way of maintaining status while gradually sliding out of the rat race. Performing such functions, you may get to be known as the Grand Old Man (or Grand Old Woman) of the corporation, bothering none and honored and loved by all.

Dear reader, although I mean all of the above seriously, don't take it too literally. I realize that most of us, who haven't ever really achieved top positions in a firm, are not candidates for the sort of semiretirement career I envisage. But the basic idea is still there for everyone who is in this position of being able to stay on with a firm past "retirement" age: less arduous work and responsibility, combined with more new enterprise and fun. If your job has not been an executive one, reflect upon what you might long have thought of undertaking in your own organization and never had time to tackle — a statistical survey of the budget and how the earned dollar is expended, or a mail-order program that had appeared too time-consuming to be worth the effort when you were frantically busy, but that always seemed as if it might work. Do it! In your spare time, think about how you might want to spend your time and talents when you actually do retire, and get a head start on it on certain nights or on weekends. If you're already engrossed with a new undertaking, be it writing, or carpentry, or painting, or music, or whatever, you'll slide into it full time at some future date much more easily if you've already dipped your feet into the water.

So the hell with power and authority! There's a host of rewarding things to undertake without them, and the bus is much less crowded in the rear.

Chapter Seven

The Home of the Slave

O LIVER GOLDSMITH HAD SOMETHING ELSE in mind
when he wrote about lovely woman stooping to folly,
but the words are extremely apt when one considers the
way so many housewives choose to spend their days in the
latter decades of their lives. They don't even have to stoop,
because they've been in that stance for so many years in
performing the necessary daily routine jobs of housekeeping
and home building.

I don't mean in any way to denigrate or underrate the
absolute importance of the tasks a good and loving wife and
mother performs for so many years. In my view her role has
usually been infinitely greater, in all the aspects that matter
most in life, than that of the worker — male or female — who
brings home the pay envelope. What is more, the challenges
of bearing and raising children intelligently, maintaining
an inspiring as well as an attractive home, cooking and serving up nutritious as well as appealing meals may well have
called forth all her strength and creativity.

But at this stage in life, let's face two things about it. The
first is that essentially she's been holding down a batch of
service jobs throughout her adulthood and, even if she had
the inclinations or the talents within her to be an Edna
St. Vincent Millay or a Billie Jean King for that matter, she's
never had time even to experiment. This may be true of

most people in most jobs, but it's particularly so of the housewife. There were always beds to be made, meals to prepare and serve, laundry to be washed, shopping to be done, windows to be cleaned, new curtains for the living room to be thought about and perhaps sewn by hand. As my brother Fred, a humorous writer, once put it: "Housework is okay, but it's tough to make a killing at it."

All this almost goes without saying, and I only particularize it to make the second point that, if you want to hang in there and live the rest of your years in an interesting and productive way, you've got to

CHANGE YOUR PRIORITIES!

For many years chores and the welfare and interests of other people simply had to be the central impulse in your daily life, probably filling almost all your waking hours. Now the time has come to step back and re-evaluate what still may be important to you and to anyone still living with you, and what really is of little concern to anyone — including you. You may be continuing to perform a host of service tasks out of pure habit. Or you may be doing so because you never stopped to think about which of them should still be shouldered through conscientiousness or love, and which should be shucked off forever. It's time to break away from the drudgery that has little or no meaning anymore, and find new and stimulating occupations that can gratify your mind and spirit, and possibly even enrich your purse. As Karl Marx said it: "You have nothing to lose but your chains!"

In many ways, the philosophy that this book is trying to

put across is even more meaningful for nonoffice working women than for men. For one thing, such women are more likely to have been facing the same general routine without change for many years, while most men and job-holding women vary their occupations from time to time over a long period. Then, the make-way-for-tomorrow syndrome, or its equivalent, is likely to hit a housebound woman earlier in life than it does a man. Both the menopause and the time when children have grown up sufficiently not to be under a mother's wing anymore are likely to have occurred before a woman is even fifty years old. Finally, since a woman's life expectancy is longer than a man's, she really has a long, open road ahead of her at the time that her situation — and, I would hope, her priorities — are altered. She well may have thirty-five or forty leftover years! That's a long, long time to spend doing tasks that once were much more meaningful than they now have become. It's really an entire and whole new life, and that's what you can and should make of it.

What am I talking about when I say that many of the once vital daily occupations ought to be re-evaluated to see if you're still undertaking them even though they've pretty well ceased to be meaningful? You ask why the details of everyday existence still don't have to be carried out, even if some circumstances have changed?

Right. Certainly they do. But not nearly to the extent that they once did. You are still going to have to continue to eat, and there's no propaganda being fostered here recommending that you live in a pig sty from now on, but you certainly can ease up to a most gratifying degree upon how much absolutely has to be done anymore, and the hours you need to devote to it all. I would venture to bet that you now can cut your household tasks at least in half, and open up many hours of each day for undertaking things that you always wanted to do, or perhaps never dreamed of trying before.

How?

Well, for one thing, the really thorough cleaning of floors, and the constant dusting of everything around a house, was, apart from esthetic considerations, a proper health precaution when babies and very young children were around. (Maybe. I once read that a certain quota of dirt, ingested and breathed in, acted as a sort of immunity in the nonsterile world we inhabit. But then, I'll admit you shouldn't believe everything you read, so let's get on with my own thesis in the hope that you will believe *this*.) We'll concede that meticulous attention to cleanliness makes sense all through the period when children are crawling on the floor and probably for quite some long time after that as well.

But now you and your husband/lover/roommate are in your forties or fifties or sixties, and I'll tell you something about the male at that age. He is really not likely to fret about an accumulation of dust in a corner or on the mantlepiece, even assuming he notices it at all. Your children never did notice it. So at this stage, it's only an exercise in masochism to leap up daily to perform an unexciting chore that doesn't have any real meaning for anyone, and specifically if its undertaking means that you have to postpone or cancel plunging into something else that will really brighten your day.

Did I hear you say that even if nobody else cares, *you* do? Fair enough: in that case, don't let me talk you out of it. If you really are so devoted a housekeeper as to be miserable if everything doesn't always look like a glossy color-spread in a woman's magazine, then you already have a daily priority that gratifies you. Don't think of giving it up because an ignorant, insensitive male author tells you to do so. But if you are not, and have only spent the many hours wearing out the vacuum cleaner and the mop and the dust rag through pure conscientiousness, just try the following technique for a while, and see if it doesn't open up a new world of extra time in which you can do what you enjoy and find satisfying.

There aren't too many luxury ships in service any more, but do you remember the way a certain type of ship's steward polices up his section of a deck? Unless there has been an orgy in one of his cabins the previous night, there's no entire stripping and remaking of a bed for him! Just a series of quick efficient yanks at the corners, a tucking in of sheets

and blankets in a single gesture, and a slapping down of a bedspread accompanied by a practiced smoothing gesture. He'll toss out dead flowers and cigarette butts, certainly, but why bother with really cleaning ashtrays — what's his moist breath and a dirty towel for except to brush them out, and give a pretty good surface impression that the cabin has been cleaned? A little more attention to the bathroom, yes, but if a glass tumbler needs drying, the same used towel that the occupant has dried his or her hands with does the job nicely. And on and out to the next cabin.

If you were in a position to watch such a steward carry out his duties that way, you might well be annoyed or disgusted or amused or all three. But the fact is that, since you're not doing the job yourself, and since the cabin looks very acceptable indeed when you return to it, you have no reason to be conscious of it, and so it doesn't bother you at all. What is more, ship travel may involve seasickness, but it has no reputation at all for laying the passengers low with the dirt diseases, such as dysentery or typhoid. A reasonable amount of cleanliness is certainly desirable, but more for esthetic reasons than sanitary ones (apart from the preparation of food, of course). Really obsessive concern to achieve truly hygienic sanitary conditions is admirable if you are a hospital orderly, but it is simple neurosis when it occupies too much of the time and effort of the mistress of an adult household. A good and thorough cleaning now and then is enough to clear your conscience and make the place look pleasantly habitable. "This room looks *lived in*" is the flattering but honest evaluation people are likely to make of an unconventionally sloppy room, and it can be a very nice compliment. You may not be of this turn of mind, and as I've said before, if you are not, God bless you. Continue to be as diligent and hard-working as you ever were. But think about it first. Are you really that house-proud, or have you been brainwashed into never relaxing from your slave tasks by tradition, your mother, your husband, or a subscription to *House Beautiful?*

Slackening off on housework isn't the only way a woman in these new circumstances can change her priorities and find time to be herself. Three square meals a day, all nutritiously planned, were part of your contribution to your young children's welfare and health. You and your man thrived on it too, and the routine of regular fixed hours for breakfast, lunch, and dinner was as sacred as the Holy Writ. Eating in agreeable company is a sociable occasion, and it may well have been a great thing for everybody, but particularly for the others. It kept you damned busy, even if you sometimes got help cleaning up.

Is it all really necessary anymore? Is it even desirable, as you get older, to have so many hearty, scheduled meals? Doctors are agreed that we ought to eat less in these years, both from the standpoint of health and of beauty. Schools and job hours used to dictate when your family had to eat, but the children are out of school now and perhaps your husband is retired. If that's the case, neither of you need be slaves to the kitchen clock any longer: Eat more simply, with less in the way of elaborate preparation (unless you feel like it on occasion), and eat when the fancy and hunger hit you. Remember that "demand feeding" is conceded to be the best way to nurse new babies, and it makes infinitely good sense that it's likely to be best for anyone whose life no longer has to be regulated by fixed hours.

For instance, think about this. Everybody wants something the first thing in the morning, but fixing a simple breakfast is no particular hassle for anyone. A matter of minutes. Forget a formal preparation of lunch altogether. Just stock the refrigerator with whatever you and whoever may be living with you likes, and raid the refrigerator whenever the moment seems right. After breakfast, at which you've probably had, at the very least, a hot beverage, no one needs more than one full hot meal a day. Save it for the convivial evening meal when, if your husband is still working, he'll want it, and if he isn't he'll join you in relishing it even more because it's the real, sit-down meal of the day.

That would be a change in your priorities that probably won't save you more than an hour or two each day, but an extra hour or two, on top of what else you can pick up, is a handy length of time, particularly when you've found something you truly enjoy doing, and want to get back to it. The household doesn't have to run like clockwork at this stage of life, and both you and anyone living in it will survive very nicely if you decide to run counter to the instincts of years and don't tend your chores as if an army sergeant had posted a duty roster for the day's program. There's always a tomorrow on which socks can be darned, or the shelves in the closet tidied, and if *today* you're simply dying to get back to that magnificent piece of embroidery that is going so well and that is not going to have any function other than to give you immense satisfaction and joy in your accomplishment, get to it! That way you'll be living good days, and not merely seeing them slip by.

Back in 1925 George Kelly (who happened to be Princess Grace Kelly's uncle) won the Pulitzer Prize for drama with his play, *Craig's Wife*. It was about a woman who was so house-proud and so house-concerned that she ruined life for everyone, including herself. Hers was an extreme case, but there's a great deal of Craig's wife inherent in many women, and it's fostered and abetted continually by magazine articles, books, and television advertising. Extreme domesticity may indeed have made good sense when a household had young children around, and without a rational and loving order running things, all might have been chaos. Taking care of the daily needs of a working husband and schoolchildren probably were your primary concerns, and it was right to take pride if you did a good job. But that's not your situation anymore, and it's time to change your priorities and stretch out to be *yourself* for once, instead of having to concentrate almost exclusively upon being of service to others. You can maintain form and order in your life, but shuck off rigidity. Try to expand your horizons and you may find out that they're limitless.

Of course, if you yourself happen to be Craig's Wife, and the impeccable household actually is the most important thing in the world to you, let's forget everything I've written here. There is one nice thing about this book or any book. If you've kept it in good condition, you can take it back to your bookstore and exchange it for another.

Chapter Eight

The Ever Young

MANY, MANY YEARS AGO when I was a teenager and, at least from the story I'm about to tell, a pretty dewy-eyed one, I read a passage from an extremely saccharine novel that impressed me enough that I then read it aloud to my considerably older brother and his friend, who happened to be in the room. It would take a good deal of inane research now to dig up a copy of A. A. Milne's *Two People* and I have no intention of undertaking it. I remember the general idea well enough, as set down in cold type by the whimsical creator of Winnie the Pooh. It was that if a person could dictate an ideal life it would be to be a famous athlete between the ages of fifteen and twenty-five; a beautiful woman from twenty-five to thirty-five; a dashing soldier-adventurer from thirty-five to forty-five; a spectacular financier from forty-five to fifty-five; a distinguished statesman from fifty-five to sixty-five; and a gardener from sixty-five to seventy-five.

I'm sure I haven't got it just right after all these years, but that's close enough. Anyhow, I read the passage aloud in a hushed and reverent voice. There was a moment's silence, and then my brother's friend said mildly, "It seems to me that there'd be more kick in it to be a famous athlete from sixty-five to seventy-five."

I had to laugh then, both ruefully at myself for my naiveté and more heartily at the humor of the comment. Today I'm not laughing. To be a gardener in those later years of life is, I'm sure, an admirable and gratifying occupation. Indeed, perhaps it's the actual best goal for you who are reading this and, if it is, you may have many of the answers to hanging in there right on tap. Gardening is a superb profession/recreation/hobby for those with a taste and a talent for it, and the fact that I, with my extremely brown thumb, happen not to be a candidate to undertake it, is not interesting to anyone but me. Go to it if gardening is, or could be, your thing. I'll even be a little envious of you because I can see the satisfactions and rewards a good gardener obtains and I'd like them for myself — if they didn't involve gardening.

The fact is that I'd actually love to be a famous athlete from sixty-five to seventy-five, but somehow I'm afraid that seems even further out of reach than becoming a gardener. Is there anything remotely comparable that isn't?

Yes, by heaven, there is! We will not win any trophies or newspaper headlines for it, but we can work — and succeed — in staying ever young in mind, in spirit, and to a gratifying extent in body as well. If we do succeed in maintaining useful bodies for ourselves, it will be more than good enough. We really are reconciled to not being an Olympic champion.

Most of us have the infirmities of aging sneak up on us over the years, one by one, and don't actually realize what's taken place until the accumulation of ailments forces us to face up to the fact that we've changed for the worse. The physical changes are the most obvious ones, but the mental ones are every bit as significant and more evident to the people around you. They may not be aware that your once supple bones are creaking, but they know very well if you, once a warm and humorous person, are now resentful and dour. If you, who used to be considerate and polite, have become aloof and arrogant. If you, who once were so aware of new ideas and movements, today close your ears to anything in the 1970s that strikes you as strange and absurd. If you who, with the rapport you had when you were younger with interesting people of all ages, have in later years turned off communication with those not of your generation.

If this has happened to you, it's chiefly your own damned fault. I don't say that young people don't often make things difficult for you to accept, but I'll bet that you did too when you were young and the shoe was on the other foot. Why not? Younger people have to try to shape the world to their own ideas. It's going to be their world and if you in your conceit — and it *is* conceit at this stage — become a stumbling block, who can blame their having some insensitivity to your feelings?

I'm not advocating your getting out of the way. The theme of this book is that you should hang in there, as long as you last, forever. But don't hang in there as a resister of everything that isn't a part of your own past experience. The world changes and you must ride along with it and become a part of it, if you're going to keep living happily and constructively. You can't turn the 1970s back into the 1940s or 1950s even if you think it would be a good idea. So fit yourself into the 1970s, and don't moan for the Good Old Days. No younger person wants to hear that sort of thing but if, instead, you become an older, experienced associate who is eager and enthusiastic about what's going on *now*, you may well find yourself welcome.

Actually, there are a number of unconstructive personal characteristics that many of us may have had throughout life. We may very well have gotten away with them because, when one is a part of an active, free-swinging community and is a vital part of it, such matters are likely to be overlooked. I am referring to things like holding the stage interminably while you deliver an opinion or tell a story, and overriding any interruptions, no matter what percentage of your audience is either falling asleep or simply politely biding the time until you will blessedly shut up. The equally objectionable antithesis is when you yourself are an interrupter. I don't know which is worse: the one makes you a bore and the other a boor.

On the other side of the coin, some elders, far from taking over the center of the stage, create an atmosphere for themselves of either withdrawal or indifference to what's going on. How often have you heard an older person say, with a shrug, something like: "Oh, well. I won't be around to see it." *Don't ever add fuel yourself* to the down-grading of senior citizens or you will deserve being on the receiving end sometimes. *Don't* make jokes about your false teeth — that's putting yourself down, along with everyone else who wears dentures. The jokes are never very funny ones and simply tend to estrange you further from people who don't have that particular problem.

There are so many unfortunate actions that older people are likely to perform needlessly, sometimes to their own detriment, that an entire catalogue could be made of them. A male example is the good old boy, accompanied by a woman near his own age, who flirts with a young waitress, while giving his order, or leaving his tip. It's insulting to his companion, and demeaning to the young woman — and to himself. A female example might be the compulsion in an older woman to undermine her daughter's authority in the daughter's own household.

The problem is that these are the sorts of characteristics that are likely to become accentuated in older years in somebody who has always been prone to display them in the past. I have been a long way from being guiltless myself in a pas-

sion to hold people paralyzed with boredom in a living room, but at least now I've done enough introspection to try to quell such habits as I become older, and like most of us, more garrulous. Try thinking about whether you could use some self-control in these areas, especially when among younger people, for if they are at all polite they are reluctant to tell you off, even if you deserve it.

Another self-defeating characteristic that often seems to become accentuated in later years with those who are inclined that way anyhow, is insisting upon proving you are right about something or the other, whether it's important or not. An example of this, and the moral to be drawn from the story, was so well told by that genius Alexander King in his utterly charming book *Peter Altenberg's Evocations of Love,* that I certainly can do no better than reprint it here, rather than try to make the point myself. The title of this particular fable is "The Proof":

Because my house was being painted, I moved for a few days into a quiet, modest hotel just around the corner from my apartment. My luggage consisted of a cigar box containing two pairs of socks and a newspaper in which I had wrapped a bottle of whiskey (just in case).

"Shall I send for your baggage?" said the bellhop after I had registered with a great flourish.

"You don't have to bother," I said. "I haven't got any."

I had to pay in advance, of course.

Around midnight I heard a funny sound in the bathroom, and a moment or two later a little mouse made its appearance. It climbed up on the bureau, inspected my meager belongings and then went down on the floor again, where it performed a few rather mystical mouse-calisthenics. Later it went back into the bathroom, where it seemed to be busy with one thing or another for the rest of the night.

When I got up in the morning I said to the chambermaid, "There is a very arrogant mouse in this room who bothered me last night."

"In this hotel there aren't any mice," said the chambermaid. "This is a first-class hotel, and everything has just been freshly painted and decorated!"

When I went downstairs I said to the elevator boy, "You've got very loyal chambermaids here. I told the girl in my room that I was bothered by a mouse last night, and she said I must have just imagined it."

"She's quite right," said the elevator boy. "There's one thing we haven't got in this hotel, and that's mice!"

My complaint must have gotten around, because the desk clerk and even the doorman gave me some very peculiar glances when I passed them — the sort of glances you give to a man who arrives in a hotel with two pairs of socks in a cigar box and a whiskey bottle wrapped in an old newspaper, and, besides that, sees mice in a hotel where there aren't any.

Another thing. My latest book of poems, *What the Day Brings Me,* had fallen out of my pocket, and the bellhop had read the title and my name on it before he handed it back to me.

So, you see, under all these circumstances my credibility as a plaintiff certainly didn't have much standing with anybody. On the other hand, my irrational behavior earned me a certain aura of eccentricity which one generally associates with the behavior of a willful child or a chronic invalid.

The mouse appeared punctually the following evening and performed his little ritualistic evolutions, until I finally made up my mind to do something about it.

On the third morning I went to a store and I bought a mouse trap and some bacon, and I carried this device ostentatiously past all the hotel personnel that happened to be on duty at that time.

When I awoke the next day, the mouse was inside the trap. I didn't plan to say anything to anybody about this. I was just going to carry the culprit downstairs and leave him at the desk as ultimate and indisputable proof of my veracity.

And then, just as I was about to leave my room, a shattering thought came to me. Wasn't I about to do something pretty silly, and perhaps even disgusting?

Yes! I was about to prove, once and for all, that *there was* a mouse in a hotel where there were *no mice.* I was about to sacrifice at one stroke my whole attractive nimbus as a man who had arrived at a hotel with two pairs of socks in a cigar box and a whiskey bottle, which was now empty. I was suddenly going to degrade myself to the status of a petty, pedantic creature who will stop at nothing to prove himself in the right.

I quickly tiptoed back into my room and released the mouse on the wide window ledge that ran all the way over onto the next roof.

When I checked out of the hotel, half an hour later, I left the empty mouse trap with the bellhop, and all the people standing around the hotel lobby had sweet, almost proprietary, smiles for me as I finally exited through the revolving door.

Now remember! If it should ever happen that *you* are absolutely right about something, and *you* can even furnish undeniable proof of it, stop and see whether this minor triumph is really worth the sacrifice of your irrational, but nevertheless rather attractive and whimsical, personality.

All of the foregoing refers to our mental attitudes and, to a great extent, it's the most important aspect of staying ever young. But let's not overlook the physical, even if we're not going to be world famous athletes in our sixties or seventies.

Obviously what I'm about to write here isn't applicable to the really unfortunate people who are struck down by an irreversible major physical calamity. I can only bare my head to those brave spirits who can sometimes hang in there in the face of cancer or a severe stroke or heart attack or a devastatingly crippling accident. The fact that there are some such can be nothing more than further inspiration to those of us to whom nothing has happened. Except that we are growing older.

More things than joints harden and stiffen as we age, and our minds and attitudes are likely to be the first and most important casualties. That's why I discussed them first. These changes in you are not so likely to be apparent to you yourself, however, as the stiffening of your neck muscles (so that you have to turn your shoulders instead of just your head to see a pretty woman), the rheumatic fingers, the fallen arches, the dental catastrophes, the dimming vision, and failing hearing. Be of good courage! Between modern medical help and your own indomitable spirit, you can lick them all!

Practically everyone in the world seems to wear glasses now, so needing them doesn't make you anything special. And while cataracts are certainly no fun, the newest techniques in operations and the use of contact lenses have a marvelous record of safety and success. Today there are lightweight arch-supporters, molded to one's feet, that not only restore comfort but get potential cripples back on their feet and even onto the tennis courts as agile as they ever were. If you choose to do so, you can get rid of gray hair rather easily. Hearing aids (I hear) are not yet perfect, but they do work and are getting better all the time, while a good dentist can really work miracles when all seems lost and you've almost resigned yourself to a lifetime of milk toast, with hash as a special treat.

But you will take advantage of medical and pharmaceutical offerings largely because it's obvious you need help in one physical area or another, and such help is available and can be bought. There will still remain the vital things that you have to do for yourself, which require effort rather than money, but which certainly pay off in enabling you to look and feel as young as you can. And that is a big part of hanging in there.

Let's concede that we're not going to be famous athletes at this age. But let's be fit and healthy, because this is a matter we really can do something about. Good nutrition, and possibly vitamin supplementation, is the first step, and right after that comes a proper, sensible exercise program.

Inexpensive government publications that are sound and authoritative are available from the Government Printing Office (these are discussed in greater detail in Chapter 12).

Other literature can be obtained, and inquiries answered, from The President's Council on Physical Fitness, 400 Sixth Street N.W., Washington, D.C. 20201. In addition, there are a number of excellent books that you can consult to your great advantage if you're going to become serious about shaping up physically, and several of the best of them almost seem ideal from the standpoint of the older person, even though they were written with people of all ages in mind.

For a somewhat surprising change has taken place in recent years in the thinking of many authorities about what is the best regimen to keep a person healthy and fit in life, and it doesn't involve violent, arduous exercise or calisthenics, as it always did in the old days. Instead, a regular, but truly rather easy program of exercises, that requires as little as one hour or less a week, tones up the physiological components of the body, such as heart and lungs and muscles, and restores flexibility to the frame, that so frequently is lost as a person grows older. It is beyond the scope of this book to outline the details of these programs, but I would recommend that you take a look at one or more of the following books, each of which sets forth a life-style of attaining good condition and then keeping physically fit, and is quite appropriate for the middle-aged and older.

Total Fitness in 30 Minutes a Week by Laurence E. Morehouse, Ph.D., with Leonard Gross. Simon and Schuster, 1975.

Type A Behavior and Your Health by Meyer Friedman, M.D., and Ray H. Rosenman, M.D. Alfred A. Knopf, 1974.

How to Save Your Life by Earl Ubell. Harcourt Brace Jovanovich, 1973.

Aerobics by Kenneth H. Cooper, M.D. Bantam Books, 1968.

This is just a partial list of books that have proved themselves wonderfully helpful to people who are either nonathletic by inclination, or have let themselves get out of shape, or whose fitness has simply declined due to the aging process. Many more exist in your bookstore or library: I am merely trying to goad you into investigating the right physical exercise program for *you*. It may be that a book on yoga or dance exercises would be your best choice.

It's quite possible that you are in good enough shape, or can achieve it, to continue to enjoy more arduous physical pursuits or even take them up. That's certainly not for all elderly people, and even lifelong tennis or golf enthusiasts should be sure to have their doctors check up on their physical condition. You should have advice about how bright the green light is that allows you to plunge ahead in active sports. Generally speaking, a tennis player turns from singles to doubles as he gets older, and limits himself to two or three sets, without any diminution of pleasure in the game. Golfers may settle for nine holes rather than eighteen, and may even give up the real exercise portion of golf — walking — by using a golf cart to traverse the course. I really can't be too enthusiastic about that, but anything that gets you out in the open, doing at least something physical, is a lot better than doing nothing at all.

I own a book of famous sports photographs of which I'm quite fond. It has pictures of events like Roger Bannister breaking the tape in the first mile ever run under four minutes and Babe Ruth pointing his bat at the section deep in center field where he was about to hit the home run that beat the Cubs in the World Series. It now contains an extra photograph that I clipped out of a periodical and taped onto the frontispiece of the book. It is a picture of the members of the Oakland, California, Women's Rowing Club, pulling away at

their oars on the waters of Lake Merritt. Every Wednesday morning these women take their places in a whaling boat and, under the smart direction of their coxswain, row with energy and precision for an hour. Every Wednesday, whether it's jolly boating weather or not.

Well, that's interesting, but why is it particularly interesting? Simply because the entire crew of the Oakland Women's Rowing Club is composed of women whose ages range from the late sixties to the eighties! Almost every one is a grandmother.

But even if you are not up to tennis or golf or rowing on Lake Merritt, you can choose a milder program that can be realistic and appealing to you. Staying fit shouldn't be a chore, and it doesn't have to be one, but it's such a vital part of hanging in there that selecting an activity — and then doing it — is a chief new priority for you to undertake. Particularly as you find yourself grunting over small exertions that never bothered you before!

A Few Questions for You to Think About

1. *Apart from physical and health considerations, do you think you're the same person you always have been?*

Your response to this question, in plain Yes_____ or No_____ terms, is absolutely basic as to whether or not you're a good prospect to hang in there, when and if the going gets tough. You simply cannot run scared of getting older — you must thumb your nose at it. We all should change through the years, of course, gaining the plus values of additional knowledge and experience, but deep inside ourselves repose the same individuals we always were. Our minds, ideas, sense of humor, originality, warmth or coldness of heart and spirit, are all likely to be completely consistent at sixty with what they were at sixteen.

If you agree that's the case, and so answered yes, the probability is that you respect and have confidence in yourself. These are the qualities that can inspire a person to be a successful hanger-in-there, often reaping rewards and fun past any he or she ever enjoyed previously.

Why would you — or anyone — reply no to the question? If you did, I'll tell you why. You've been brainwashed. Present-day society has created and spread the point of view that aging is nothing but a problem and, what is more, a problem for everybody. The person growing older is put onto the shelf as the solution to making way for tomorrow, which certainly poses a problem for him or her. That sort of person looks ahead with despair to the prospect of years of doing nothing except idiotically passing the time idly. On the other side there are people who feel a family or a social obligation for these encumberances, whom they helped create. They now have the economic problem of supporting them out of a sense of duty. No wonder, as things are, aging seems nothing but a problem.

Did you happen to see the full back page advertisement that *Playboy* ran in the February 2, 1977, issue of the *New York Times?* I rather hope not, because the *Times* is usually read at breakfast and it may well have given you indigestion all that day. The advertisement pictured a young man identified as a senior sales representative for a major national business corporation, who is described as being typical of today's "life-embracing young adults," further delineated later in the ad as "the most vibrant group of prospects American business has been blessed with since the post-World War II generation." (Of course the basic message is that there are over 13 million of these vibrators who read *Playboy* and devour its advertising like a catalogue.)

Well, this fellow and his "millions of colleagues" deliver themselves of a number of philosophies that I won't bother you with, since they're not worth bothering about. But listen to this particular one: "To me a travel bargain is someplace the old folks don't go. I'm willing to pay a lot for that."

!!!!

With one sweeping declaration this "vital spending group" whose "lust is for life" rules out of further consideration ever visiting any of the great capital cities of the world with their museums, theaters, concerts, ballets, operas, and historic architectural gems. They will have to avoid like the plague every beautiful, romantic resort that has won a reputation simply because it *is* outstandingly beautiful and romantic. They had better stay away from any location where a popular, lively event is taking place: there are sure to be quite a number of old folks at Mardi Gras in New Orleans or at the Kentucky Derby or at Wimbledon.

Does all this require any further editorial comment? I

think not. The statement speaks eloquently enough, I'm afraid, for a great number of young adults, in managerial positions, who may be the ones who'll be controlling your future destiny. Let's just accept that and go on.

The older person today is consistently being disenfranchised from the citizenship to which he has always belonged — a citizenship whose foundation is the work ethic. If and when the time comes that a person is treated this way, he or she becomes someone who no longer matters to the community, and public denigration will inevitably grow into a demeaning of one's own self-respect. But the real truth is that it is only in comparatively recent years that the elderly have come to be regarded as nothing more than a nuisance. Through history they were invariably respected, and even revered as fonts of wisdom. Leaders, from industry to government, were seldom chosen from the ranks of the Young Turks but rather from the ranks of the experienced and proven. That invariably made them just about the age that today will earn them little more than mandatory retirement. Everything is geared to separate the elderly from the rest of the world and isolate them from any real activities.

A number of people are now trying to fight back and turn this tide, such as the "gray power" lobby and other groups, but even if and when their efforts bear fruit, changes may come too little and too late for you. Besides, if you are truly intent upon hanging in there, it's the appeal to your own individual spirit and competence that's the exciting and challenging one. If you can't change the world, don't let the world change you. Your external circumstances may, and probably will change, but not necessarily for the worse. An ordered, never-changing existence can be dull. Remember how Thoreau put it? "If a man does not keep pace with his companions, perhaps it is because he hears a different drummer. Let him step to the music which he hears, however measured or far away."

2. Are you in reasonably good health?

_____ Yes _____ No

Admittedly there is no gainsaying the fact that, even if you have a marvelously indomitable spirit, the physical debilitation that so frequently sets in as we grow older can cripple your high resolve. The loss of limbs or organs or senses or just great constant pain is surely enough reason for anyone to decide to lay down his arms and quit the active world. And yet . . . and yet . . . I would want your answer to the original question still to be yes under any but the most impossibly tragic circumstances (such as are laid out in the small print in accident insurance policies as enabling the insured to collect double the face value).

The will to overcome physical handicaps and the ability to surmount them are things that take place so frequently and so universally that while they're always inspiring to read about, we are not astounded. Too many world figures have offered us brilliant examples, from Beethoven's deafness to Franklin Delano Roosevelt's polio, from Patricia Neal's apparently hopeless stroke to Milton's blindness. But countless simple people, of no particular name or fame, have displayed the same sort of unconquerable spirit and have achieved equally inspiring great results within the frameworks of their own lives.

So, even if you have some major incapacity or pain, with all understanding and sympathy and love, I urge you not to disqualify yourself from hanging in there because of that.

3. Are you ABLE to change your priorities after all this time?

Yes_____ No_____

If you feel yes, indeed you can, you can skip the rest of this particular section and turn to the next chapter. You're already on my team and you even have my vote to be captain.

Perhaps you're not sure. Let's not kid ourselves: Some people cling tenaciously to old habits and old knowledge, and consciously or unconsciously refuse to move with the times at all. Feeling that a successful background of experience means that they know more than newcomers to the game, they fail to appreciate that the game they're now up against has some new rules. Fresh ideas ranging from the political to the spiritual jostle aside old ones. Whether they're better or not is not the point: You will become an old fogy if you don't know about them and take them into account in your thinking and your involvement. You may discard the immense growth of a new popular enthusiasm as being no more than a fad that will pass, but don't be too certain that you are right until you learn as much about it as your experience has taught you about former quasi-revolutionary ideas or movements. New technologies constantly make the old expert obsolescent if he or she doesn't keep up with what's taking place *now*. If you fall in this category of being a person who's uncertain of his ability to change, but are reading this paragraph thoughtfully and in the spirit of constructive self-evaluation, you're already on the road to being able to answer yes to the question about your ability to change priorities.

But if you vehemently said no, perhaps accompanied by a violent swear word or two, I can only express regret and encourage you to reconsider. Do you know why the famous adage "You can't teach an old dog new tricks" is not to be found in Bartlett's *Familiar Quotations?* It's because it's utter nonsense, and Bartlett knew it.

Part Three

Fights for the Fearless and Goals for the Eager

Chapter Nine

Forty Years On

THE PURSUIT OF HAPPINESS. It was considered one of man's unalienable rights by the writers of the Declaration of Independence. Yet as an accepted goal that one would think everybody would strive for, it's lost some of its zing among those who consider themselves sophisticated realists. I suppose there's ample reason for cynicism these days, considering what we have witnessed in world affairs, but take comfort. As we grow older the world will be pushing us out of its affairs more and more.

Fortunate us! Now, as the opportunity lessens for us to capture the goals that have replaced happiness in world affairs — money, power, stardom, for example — perhaps we will have time to concentrate upon simply attaining some good, old-fashioned happiness.

Admittedly, happiness isn't the only objective for people who make the determination to hang in there. First, one has to survive. But after that, without happiness, survival loses most of its point. Prisoners with life sentences survive. So will you, if you choose to do nothing with your latter years beyond trying to keep yourself awake through the day so that you can sleep at night. It really isn't enough.

The idea of happiness is a romantic one, perhaps, and romance isn't chic today. But let me confess. I've been an incurable romantic all of my life, and I'm wildly grateful for the happiness it has afforded me. Now, as my own hanging-in-there years approach, I'm convinced that I should continue to be the same sort of man more than ever, from this time forward, through the rest of my days. By "romance," I do not mean fairy tales or soap operas, but instead that sort of romantic spirit that thrilled me in the words of a song we sang when I was a student some forty-odd years ago. It was called "Forty Years On" and the second verse contained these lines:

> *God give us grace to be strong and beleaguer,*
> *Games to play out whether earnest or fun,*
> *Fights for the fearless and goals for the eager,*
> *Twenty and thirty and forty years on!*

The tune was a stirring one, but the thing that stirred this romantic schoolboy — and still does now that the intervening forty years are an actuality — were the words. It was a rallying call and an inspiration to fight the good fight throughout all one's life, and never to be beaten or lose the wonderful human spark of ambition. It was romantic as all hell, and I found it inspiring. I still do.

The only difference is that back then I thought it a valorous concept, but could only accept it on romantic faith. Today I know that it is true. The older we grow, the more vital it is to continue to have games to play out and fights and goals. Anything less and we wither on the vine, desperately seeking ways to pass the time.

When Oliver Wendell Holmes, Jr., was ninety years old in 1931, he made a birthday speech on the radio. In it he said: "The riders in a race do not stop short when they reach the goal . . . The race is over, but the work never is done while the power to work remains. The canter that brings you to a standstill need not be only coming to rest. It cannot be, while you still live. *For to live is to function. That is all there is in living.*"

"But," you may reply, "even if I accept that as a valid statement, where does it leave me? I have no idea where to seek out functions, let alone games, or fights, or goals. Stop giving me a pep talk and tell me what I can *do!*"

Perhaps I can best start by giving examples of what so many other staunch (and romantic) people have done. Some have been world renowned geniuses endowed with extraordinary talent, but many more are just ordinary folks. The list of men and women of extremely ripe years, whose performances in an infinite variety of fields have been as good or better than almost anyone else in the world, could be the inspiring subject of a complete book in itself. A few of the most obvious names that instantly come to mind would include Michelangelo, who didn't even begin his magnificent and obviously backbreaking work on St. Peter's cathedral until he was over seventy and actually died at age eighty-nine while still putting on his final touches.

Similarly, Frank Lloyd Wright did much of his very best and most creative work at the same stage of his life. He designed the Guggenheim Museum in New York, surely one of the most imaginative architectural edifices of our times, shortly before his death, which took place when he was ninety-one years old.

Grandma Moses was a farmer before she first began to paint, and that was when she was almost eighty. From then on, nothing could stop her right up to the time of her death: age one hundred. Other great artists who continued to do wonderfully vigorous and productive work to the very end, at comparable ages, were Pablo Picasso and Marc Chagall.

In the world of music, what can compare with Artur Rubinstein's incredible recital at Carnegie Hall when, at eighty-nine, he brought off an evening at the piano, playing as brilliantly as ever, despite not being able to read the music or even see the keyboard clearly, due to his failing sight. Giuseppe Verdi composed a couple of his most notable operas in his late seventies and, in the jazz field, Duke Ellington was making brilliant recordings right up to his death at a similar age.

Great statesmen are likely to go on longer than most since, at least until comparatively recently, they have been likely not to attain center stage until they've reached the sort of age at which industry would be apt to toss them out. They do not stay there too long, however, unless they show immense vitality and leadership, but so many of them have done so that we can all take heart from their records of productive longevity. Whether you admire all of them or not as leaders of states, you cannot deny that Mohandas Gandhi, Benjamin Franklin, Charles de Gaulle, Golda Meir, Mao Tse-tung, Eamon de Valera, and many others were mighty proficient at the art of hanging in there.

Many eminent authors have shown us that, far from throwing in the towel at an advanced age and pawning their typewriters, they produced some of their best work on the far side of age seventy-five. Baroness Karen Blixen was one, along with Leo Tolstoi, George Bernard Shaw, Margaret Mead, Victor Hugo, P. G. Wodehouse, and Bertrand Russell. Russell, as a matter of fact, went far past his writing at the age of ninety when he continued to be the spearhead of the nuclear disarmament movement. And who can overlook Albert Schweitzer, who began the quest for world peace that won him the Nobel Peace Prize when he was seventy, and who personally attended his patients in his hospital at Lambaréné, Gabon, right up to the time of his death at ninety years of age?

The list of internationally eminent people who maintained their vigor and capabilities right through their long lives could go on almost endlessly. Paul Dudley White, the eminent heart specialist, conducted an active medical program right up to his death in his nineties. The performing arts would claim many: Maurice Chevalier, Mae West, the Lunts, and John Wayne, are just a few that come to mind. Helena Rubinstein and Coco Chanel were each dominant figures in the beauty and fashion worlds all the way until their respective deaths just on one side or the other of age ninety. Nothing stops the indomitable except death itself. But while the citing of famous people who had indomitable spirit is rousing, that spirit is not the province alone of the spectacularly gifted. You and I have it tucked away inside us, but we have to be aware that it's there to be called upon and nurtured.

So let's turn from the sublime — but not to the ridiculous — and take a look at people whose eminence does not put them in a special category. Let's look at the sort of things they found to do at age levels where society is prone to tell them to creep to the attic and perhaps some time before dark a bowl of warm oatmeal will be sent upstairs.

In South Norwalk, Connecticut, a man named Hoyt Catlin became sixty-five in 1956, after a long and successful engineering career. He had also been a patent inventor, but if there was one thing that he had not particularly done well at, it was gardening. In his own words, Mr. Catlin confesses to having more than a brown thumb. He claims a black thumb.

Today, in his late eighties, he is the most vital, gregarious, and rewardingly occupied of men. He must have been a wizard in the flush of his youthful exuberance at age sixty-five, when he founded Fertl, Inc., in South Norwalk, which produces a cube of soil containing flower or vegetable seeds. Planted in pots indoors during the colder weather in the early spring, these begin their growth and then are transplanted to outdoor gardens when the weather becomes warmer.

All this is interesting enough insofar as it concerns Hoyt Catlin's ability to change his priorities, and create a new successful latter-day occupation for himself. But even more gratifying has been the story of who his employees have been, and are. Quite by chance he happened to hire some senior citizens at the very beginning, and he found out that they not only performed well, but had a superior record of less absenteeism and employee turnover than younger employees in comparable firms. The result has been that today the average age of a Fertl, Inc., employee is sixty-eight, and the company has many workers in their seventies, eighties, and even a few in their nineties. Since sixty-eight is the average age, that means the staff includes many younger workers as well, and age seems to be no barrier to Fertl's people working happily and cooperatively side by side. The firm is a spectacular example of how beautifully older people can continue to hang in there, if given the opportunity.

Another former engineer who shifted gears magnificently is Eva Hirdler Greene, of Costa Mesa, California. For almost four decades Mrs. Greene was in the mining and petroleum engineering field and then, in her early sixties, she launched her own testing and evaluation business. It has proved valuable enough that it is still going strong now, thirty years later, and Mrs. Greene is still running it herself. Of course, she is only ninety-one years old!

Then there is Clement Lee, of San Diego, California, who found out that no one wanted to hire a man of his age any longer, when he reached his mid-seventies, despite the fact that he felt as well as ever and had enjoyed a career that showed his versatility and accomplishments. Mr. Lee had been a reporter on the *Denver Post,* a navy security guard, a professional musician who played the clarinet and the saxaphone, and a law court reporter but, a few years ago, his efforts to find work seemed to indicate that he had become unemployable, simply because of his age.

So he and his wife, Grace, who had been married fifty years, decided that they could make a useful contribution toward improving the fast deteriorating American environment, and took to the road. Each day the Lees drive along California interstate highways in search of beer and soft drink cans, tossed from car windows by thoughtless automobile travelers, and pick up other such trash as well. They don't have to hunt very hard. Sometimes they collect as many as five hundred cans a day, which they then sell to a salvage dealer for recycling, and regardless of what money they may or may not make, they take immense satisfaction in knowing that they are doing more than their share toward a better national environment.

The Texas Refinery Corporation in Fort Worth instituted its Sizzling Sixties Club for people sixty years old and over, some twenty years ago. It's been a wild success with some four hundred members today, for these senior salespeople have invariably turned out to be the very best sellers the corporation has. Adlai M. Pate, Jr., the company's president and board chairman, is quoted as follows: "I'm grateful for what I consider the shortsighted policies of firms that enforce mandatory retirement of older employees. Every time they let someone go because of age, I have another potential salesperson and good salespeople, like good wines, get better with age."

Mrs. Lucille McCormick of Flint, Michigan, is a black woman, a former elementary school teacher who, past eighty now, is finding more joy and purpose in her life than ever before. Throughout her teaching career she found she was most effective with young people on a one-to-one basis, so now, as a volunteer youth worker, she concentrates upon being a Big Sister to one child at a time, and this involves everything from tutoring children in schoolwork, to taking them to country carnivals and riding with them on roller coasters. She says that the images that some parents set are often so low in caliber that the child really has nothing to give him a pride in his heritage, and has nothing to look forward to for the future. Mrs. McCormick tries to supply the one by telling her youthful friends about Mary McLeod Bethune, Dr. George Washington Carver, W. E. B. DuBois, and other distinguished blacks whom she actually knew personally, and supplies the other by her own example and precepts. She once said: "Children need an image, and I think I can help some of them find it." Clearly she has done so, for several of her former students, who came from extremely disadvantaged homes, have become exemplary and successful citizens.

Dr. J. W. Morris of McCory, Arkansas, and Dr. Walter A. Griffin of Sharon, Massachusetts, are both practicing physicians but would otherwise seem to have little in common except for one thing. They are both one hundred years old and keep regular office hours. Dr. Griffin gave up tennis at ninety-two and driving a car at ninety-six (the latter means that he had to stop making housecalls) but Dr. Morris still does so. He explains that some patients simply can't get to his office: They are too old.

In Wheeling, West Virginia, a small group of senior citizens have banded together into an organization they call the We Fix It Committee. In the very few years of its existence, the committee has performed well over a thousand minor repair jobs for people in the area, such as work on automobile and electrical problems, carpentry and plumbing, plastering, typing, and clothing alterations. They have had no conflict with unions because the union members are glad to be relieved of these small jobs that take time away from their being able to earn much larger profits on major industrial assignments. The committee does point out to anyone else who may be inspired to do what this Wheeling group is doing that they should protect themselves by being sure that the employing person and the fixer have liability insurance, which is inexpensive and in any case is frequently included in the "homeowners policy" that most homeowners carry.

Jules Strauss is in his mid-eighties and is regarded as probably New York's most proficient paintbrush cleaner, which happens to be a quite skilled and demanding art. Apparently, with fine artists' brushes, you don't just toss them into a can of turpentine and hope for the best next time, which has been my own, admittedly unsuccessful system on the few occasions when I've tried to paint. Mr. Strauss's brush laundry is going so strong that he can't handle all the work himself, and he employs a full-time assistant.

Perhaps you already know about Marion Rice Hart? She has had quite a lot of publicity ever since she took up airplane flying in 1945 when she was fifty-two years old. Eight

years later, at sixty, she flew her plane across the Atlantic, and since then she has done it another seven times, the last quite recently when she was eighty-three, by which time she had earned the sobriquet of "the flying granny." She says she does her flying simply because she loves it and likes to go places, and on that last flight, "just for kicks," she went on to Pakistan, Bangladesh, and Ceylon.

Finally, we encounter the name of a man whom we know from past accomplishments. But in this particular episode, performed at a time well past his active career, he simply acted as an elderly person who wouldn't permit his age to disassociate him from involvement.

For decades, in this country, E. B. White was known as possibly the most graceful essayist of our time. Few writers commanded the admiration and affection that his *New Yorker* pieces elicited, and when he retired from active writing a number of years ago, many of us, who never actually knew him, experienced the same sadness as if we had lost a close friend.

So what a joy it was to pick up our copy of the *New York Times* on Tuesday morning, June 15, 1976, and see a front-page story, accompanied by a photograph, bearing the headline: E. B. WHITE TAKES ON XEROX AND WINS.

The seventy-six-year-old author had written very little in recent years, but when *Esquire* published an article by Harrison E. Salisbury that was sponsored by Xerox, he says, "It made me jump, and when I jump, I jump in the direction of a typewriter." So he fired off a letter to his favorite local newspaper, the *Ellsworth American*, which chiefly concentrates upon the neighborhood news in and around the section of the country where Mr. White now lives, Brooklin, Maine. He termed this type of arrangement, which had

Xerox pay *Esquire* to commission Mr. Salisbury to write an article, "ominous" and a threat to a free press, even though the actual article itself, "Travels Through America," seemed innocent enough. But Mr. White went on to explain why he felt so strongly, in words that showed he had lost none of his skill as an embattled essayist. He said that sponsorship in the press was an invitation to corruption and abuse. He didn't want IBM or the National Rifle Association providing him with a funded spectacular when he next opened his paper, even though a funded article might well be a tempting morsel both for a publication and a writer. He wanted to read what the editor and publisher managed to dig up on their own — and paid for out of the till.

When Mr. W. B. Jones, director of communications for Xerox and a long-time admirer of E. B. White's, heard of the letter to the *Ellsworth American,* he asked White for an elaboration of his views. The result, to everyone's lasting credit, was that Xerox abandoned two planned similar projects with other magazines and writers, and thanked Mr. White for "telling them what they did not want to hear," and for helping them reach what they now were convinced was the right decision.

E. B. White was pushing eighty when he battled successfully with one of the greatest corporations of this country. Long live E. B. White!

Chapter Ten

Do You Plan Your Vacations?

D ID YOU EVER HEAR OF AN ORGANIZATION that has
nine million members and is growing every day? Nine
million! Well, there is one with headquarters in Washington, D.C., with branches all over the country. It is the American Association of Retired Persons (AARP), and anyone
fifty-five years of age or older can join it by paying a three-
dollar annual fee, in return for which a really remarkable
variety of excellent, bargain-rate opportunities is made
available. These include everything from quality, cut-rate
pharmaceuticals and vitamins, to excellent low-cost health
and medical insurance, educational opportunities, domestic
and foreign charter flights and vacations, and more ways to
recoup your three dollars a hundredfold each year than you
could believe possible.

AARP is a nonprofit, nonpartisan, social-welfare, educational, philanthropic, and scientific organization incorporated
under the laws of the District of Columbia. It is dedicated to helping all older men and women achieve independence, dignity, and purpose, and your membership fee
also brings you its extremely professional and interesting bimonthly magazine, *Modern Maturity,* six times a year in the
mails. If you are fifty-five or older, the whole deal strikes me
as one of the very best three-dollar investments you could
possibly make in an era when three dollars won't even get
you into a first-run movie theater.

Yet AARP has a separate division called Action for Independent Maturity (AIM), whose aim and purpose are even more solidly aligned to the topic of this book. AIM's membership is open to all persons from the ages of fifty through sixty-four who are *not* yet retired, but who are smart enough and ambitious enough to start nailing a rug to the floor before the one they are standing on gets yanked out from under them. AIM has an enrollment of 350,000 people, some of whom join as individuals, but the majority do so rather as members of a group enrolled along with other members of an enlightened business organization. Annual dues once again are three dollars, and a subscription to a differently-slanted but equally admirable bimonthly magazine, *Dynamic Maturity*, is part of the deal. The business companies who offer the AIM seminars to their employees include all kinds of organizations, from small personal ones to such giants as those listed in *Fortune*'s five hundred corporations. The seminars and the literature prepare the active worker during the final fifteen years of his or her employment for the time when a mandatory retirement may set in and attempt to inspire that person to go on to future rewarding years.

For retirement should be a *reward* for a lifetime spent essentially working for a living. But it's no reward to be bored the rest of your life, which is what happens to most people who don't have something stimulating to pursue once they have lots of leisure time. Leisure time that you can use to do creative things that intrigue you is a reward: simply having unused and unimaginative spare time is not. AIM's objective is to prepare the potential retiree for the rewarding time that can be achieved.

I visited the AARP and AIM offices in Washington (1909 K Street N.W., Washington, D.C. 20049) as a part of the research for this book and was immensely impressed by a statement that one of my most cooperative hosts made. He said that everyone who takes even as little as a week's vacation, and certainly everyone who takes a much more extensive one, thinks about and discusses and plans for it long in advance, down to the smallest detail. But although the years of retirement can well be one quarter of a person's entire life, the majority of people don't give it a second's serious or constructive thought until the moment it is upon them. That may well be too late. Good performance comes from good training, and you must develop new, satisfying life-styles *before* retirement. Obviously you have to include thinking about financial needs, where you will live, health programs, hobbies and projects, but most of all you have to create a positive *attitude* about aging.

A part of AIM's retirement planning seminars involves testing your awareness of desirable attitudes and role adjustments. A few samples of the questions asked follow, and I am especially grateful to AIM for free access to their materials, and the right to use and adapt as I see fit.

You are supposed to decide whether "true" or "false" is the nearest correct answer to each question, except for the last multiple-choice one. Think what your own answers would be before reading further.

1. The further you get into retirement, the happier you are likely to be.

2. Your attitude toward work influences your attitude toward retirement.

3. Most of your fears and worries are serious and legitimate.

4. Most couples over sixty are still sexually active.

5. Young and old people have few bonds in common.
6. It takes more effort in retirement to make and keep friends.
7. No single activity will satisfy the need for quality and quantity in leisure.
8. Recognition in retirement is not important.
9. People in their seventies and eighties should avoid sports.
10. A second career can provide which of the following? (Interests, Income, Activity, Status).

Have you done your homework? Now check your reactions against the decisions that AIM came to as the result of that organization's vast experience.

1. The nearer you get to retirement, the more *you may* react negatively to it. But the further you get into retirement, the happier you're likely to be.
2. It has a great deal to do with it. If you got most of your prestige and pleasure from your work, you may find it hard to adjust. But if work was boring, you might look forward to the release and relaxation of retirement.
3. A comprehensive University of Wisconsin study says that 40 percent of our normal worries don't ever happen, some 30 percent concern those that happen and we can't change, and some 22 percent are petty and needless worries of little consequence. This leaves 8 percent of fears and worries that are legitimate — why waste your energy on the other 92 percent?
4. A Duke University study reported that 81 of the 149 married couples were still sexually active, with 10 percent of them having sexual relations more than once a

week. Cessation of sex isn't physical; invariably it's psychological.

5. They should be more allies than enemies, for the same values that discriminate against the one discriminate against the other. Both belong to age groups adjacent to the one that controls the nation and are frequently expected to be both grateful and at least moderately subservient. The young and old have much to teach and learn from each other, as well as a need for each other, so don't think in terms of a generation gap when relating to young people, but rather in terms of how much you have in common.

6. Whether it's harder or not, you should make the effort because, as Dr. Samuel Johnson once said, "If a man does not make new acquaintances as he advances through life, he will soon find himself alone." So seek people who have common interests and activities, and you're bound to find them in clubs, associations, classes, and any special interest group that you yourself find appealing.

7. True. Meet any challenges and take advantage of any opportunities. There are as many in later years as there were in earlier ones if you're receptive to them, and now you have additional experience, knowledge, and wisdom.

8. This one is both true and false. Samuel Butler once wrote that all animals except man know that the chief business of life is to enjoy it. On the other hand, it is part of human nature to like to be regarded highly, and you still can achieve that even if you have had to stop being Mr. or Madam Big. Let's say you select a hobby

that pleases and occupies you. That may be enough in itself, but if you really have the drive and intensity to become known as an expert at it, you'll get the recognition that your ego may require. How far you want to go, and how capable you may be of going that far, is a matter of relative values. You may well be happier doing no more than quietly enjoying your hobby.

9. You are never too old for active sports, assuming you have no physical handicaps that are crippling or dangerous to your health. The Senior World Championship Competitions are held in Los Angeles and include archery, badminton, basketball, cycling, bowling, decathlon, diving, fencing, golf, horseshoe pitching, ice skating, karate, marathon, rugby, soccer, softball, table tennis, tennis, and cross-country running. Most participants are in their fifties and sixties, but others are over seventy and there are some who are even in their eighties.

10. Obviously a second career can provide any one of the choices, and any one alone may be all that you're seeking. Equally obviously, it's possible that it can provide all four of the choices. I hope it does for you.

AARP and AIM are by no means the only organizations whose mission is to help people meet the financial and psychological uncertainties of aging and retirement, whether forced or not. Retirement Living Inc., a division of the Whitney Communications Corporation, publishes a magazine, *Retirement Living*, which is geared to the needs and aspirations of both people who have already retired and those who are still working but see retirement on the horizon. They do not run seminars, like AIM, but many business organizations and individuals subscribe to the magazine and also use their numerous booklets and newsletters. Retirement Living Inc. maintains offices at 150 East 58th Street, New York, N.Y. 10022, and further information and orders for these publications can be addressed there.

Other similarly motivated organizations include the National Council on the Aging at 1828 L Street N.W., Washington, D.C. 20036; the Retirement Planning and Counseling Association at 362 Atlanta Drive, Pittsburgh, Pennsylvania 15228; Manpower Education Institute (MEI) at 127 East 35th Street, New York, N.Y. 10016; and Retirement Advisers Inc. (RAI), 720 Fifth Avenue, New York, N.Y. 10019. Additionally, all over the country retirement advisory courses are offered by the adult education branches of universities and by area community colleges.

So much literature on the subject exists in the field — books, pamphlets, portfolios — that you could call it an overabundance. If that's the case you might well ask why I, who am not a professional psychologist or an economist, or a geriatrician, think I have anything of value to add. A good question, and while I can only hope my answer would be equally good, I know it's sincere and full of personal conviction. Here it is.

Whether the practical guides you find to read or listen to are helpful or not — and many of them are excellent — not one is worth much more than a tinker's dam unless you first have tuned your mind to be positive about what you're facing, to gain some assurance about how stimulating it can be, and to be convinced that far from being frightening it can be both exciting and rewarding to

CHANGE YOUR PRIORITIES

Telling you how you can best spend a limited income or where the climate is good for arthritis, or how to wile your time away on a hobby or travel is all well and good. The time will probably come when you will want to take advantage of the information of this sort that's offered in books and in courses, but if you don't prepare your mind and attitudes first about yourself and the sort of person you've always been and still are, it's putting the cart before the horse. If you are going to turn to a new approach to life in your later years, as just about all of us must, the initial step is to lift your eyes to the hills, flex your muscles, and stiffen your spine. Then and only then will you be properly ready to examine and think about the vast possibilities from which to choose, and that is where certain of the practical guidebooks may be exactly what you'll find invaluable. But first, become convinced that you not only want to hang in there, but that you damned well can!

There is a prevalent attitude in many people that they carry throughout their entire lives — an understandable but an erroneous one. It embodies the idea that life ideally should be easygoing and comfortable, and that maximum enjoyment of it is when those circumstances exist 100 percent of the time. No one would contest that one of the goals of existence is to achieve such comfort, but there's more fallacy than truth in thinking that that in itself is enough. You can't settle for just that. The joys in life come from experience and from doing things, and the most gratifying rewards spring from accomplishment. Being in the position of taking it easy when you choose is dandy and a part of the rewards, but it's something like savoring a hot dog and a drink at the half-time period of a sports event. That's not the major reason why you came.

We all have a tendency, at least upon occasion, to shrug our shoulders about extending ourselves to carry out even a pleasing prospect. We decide it isn't worth it. On a hot summer day, even though you may be very close to a beach, you decide that it isn't worth it to go through the trouble of getting there and back. An attractive invitation is extended to you for an evening but you're a little bit tired from the day and decide that it isn't worth the fun you might have to stay up that late. You meet someone whom you find very attractive, and the feeling seems mutual, but when you realize that he or she lives in Westchester County, and you are in New York City, the twenty-five mile trip strikes you as being more than it's worth. As a native New Yorker, you've always wanted to do certain things that most visitors to the city manage to take in during a weekend stay, such as wandering around Chinatown, going to the top of the Empire State building, attending a symphony concert in Lincoln Center, picnicking in Central Park, and renting a boat to go out on the lake, or whatever. But you never do. It isn't worth it.

Perhaps it's true that in some cases, it wouldn't have been worth it, but haven't you found that whenever you pressed yourself to do things under such circumstances, it *has* been worth it? You can't sit back forever in an armchair and expect the good things in the world to wander in through the door and cuddle up by your feet. You must stir yourself enough to go out and meet them.

As you age, it becomes more and more necessary to foster a positive attitude about your continuing to seek the best promise that life holds — the sense of being *alive*. If the time comes when no one either expects or wants performance from you, you will muster the courage and initiative yourself to see to it that you continue performing in the arena, and not just be a spectator. Perhaps you can do so in the same field as you always did, or an allied one, and if that's what you want — fine. No problem. But many of us either won't be able to carry on that way or, perhaps even better, are intrigued by the chance to try a new beginning. So in that case

CHANGE YOUR PRIORITIES

and set a new course for yourself. Maybe it will work out wonderfully. Maybe it won't, and then you'll just turn to something else. The world is full of a wonder of things, and success isn't the only gauge of measurement. As long as you have the will to hang in there and *try* really to live, you'll be way ahead of the person who settles for Old Rocking Chair and a steady flow of chicken noodle soup.

Some Questions for You to Think About

1. *Do you feel that a person must be endowed with un-usual strength, health, and talents, in order simply to have the will to function effectively in latter-years' life?*

Perhaps you answered yes to this one, but if you did you didn't grasp the very clear message that the stories in Chapter 9 conveyed. The same spirit of meeting each new day as a new opportunity existed in equal balance both in the geniuses discussed there and in the ordinary citizens. Courage and the will to get the most out of life are not at all the special preserves of the gifted. You and I have them too, perhaps in varying extents but certainly enough of them to make a better life out of a potentially drab one.

If you answered no, as I would certainly hope you would have if you've gotten this far into the book, turn to the next question, please.

2. *Even if you're convinced that you have the spirit to be willing to change your priorities, have you a certain hopelessness that you just don't know where to start looking?*

Yes___ No___

We need only consider this matter if you said yes, in which case you ought first to think about what your interests have been in the past, and by that I mean not only those you have actually pursued, but those you may even have once wistfully considered and not acted upon.

What activities within your community have you ever liked or admired, whether you participated in them or not?

Local politics? Club organizations, ranging from social and card-playing to gardening, literary discussion groups, or sports?

Perhaps you once had a hobby, maybe as far back as your schooldays, that you enjoyed a lot but have put aside ever since. Did you once use a camera a lot and develop, print, and enlarge your own pictures? Were you a radio ham? Were you forced to take piano lessons when you were ten, and hated it, but are regretful now that you are unable to play? Chapter 13 does not pretend to cover the field but it does set forth a wide choice of hobbies that may inspire you to start up with an old one again or to develop a new one.

Think about your skills — those you know you have, and those that are latent simply because you never called upon them. Would you be good at researching, ghost writing, bookkeeping, copy checking, painting, teaching, crafts? Many skills involve special aptitudes that an employer does not require on a full-time basis, so there are always free-lance jobs for people who have those aptitudes. They work flexibly on a part-time basis, and this might be just what would suit you. Also, be flexible in your thinking about what you can do, and don't merely think in stereotypical terms about what you may have done in the past. Think about what is available and wanted today, and believe in your ability to change your priorities and do well in a new field.

But where do you find jobs? Look for them! And don't give up if you're not successful right away, for not only do jobs exist but they also can be invented. There are definite advantages for employers in having some services performed on a part-time basis, as has been pointed out, and other advantages in using older people for them. Older people are likely to be more stable and reliable, have fewer family complications, and are more anxious to stick with a job once they land it. So scan the want ads in your daily newspapers thoroughly, *keeping a flexible mind about what you might do,* and look through the yellow pages in your telephone directory in the same spirit. Let everyone know that you're eager to work, both in conversation with friends and in letters to business organizations where you feel you might have something to contribute. That last is what is meant by inventing a job for yourself. If, for example, you are a good typist, there are always free-lance typing jobs looking for you. If you are fluent in a language, perhaps you could tutor, read foreign manuscripts for a publisher, or even try your hand at translations. And any person with sales experience in one line is apt to be good at other types of selling so, if that happens to be your talent, don't confine your job-searching to the field with which you've been familiar in the past. Salespeople are always needed, both on a full-time and part-time basis, and sometimes when a job does not exist an imaginative person can invent one and make it pay. Here is an example of what I mean, which I was privileged to witness at close hand.

I have an older brother, John, who, as the result of his boss's son graduating from college and taking over his advertising job, was forcibly "retired" when he was in his very early sixties. He had little in the way of financial reserves, so he moved to a comparatively inexpensive locality in Florida and started to try to scratch around for a living. For quite a long time, things did not go well and he had severe money troubles. He did land jobs, but they were either short-lived because the firms that hired him didn't last, or they were unproductive. Then, one day, John "invented" a job.

As an advertising man, he knew a good deal about printing. He found a job printer in his locality and explained his idea to him. If the printer would make up some handsome business cards and explanatory literature about the service that John proposed to establish, he would then bring that printer the first results of whatever he might successfully achieve. For John's idea was to establish himself as a "print-ing consultant," and to be the liaison between a company that required any printing work to be done and the printer. He knew enough about printing to be able to judge good work, compare prices, and recommend what sort of job might best suit his customers' needs. He had his own car, and so could act as a daily go-between, taking orders from a business concern, delivering them the same day to the printer, and picking up and delivering by hand when the work was ready. For these services, valuable to both parties, he received a commission on the cost of the job done.

At first he just sent out letters and rang doorbells, picking up a job here and there. But with the passage of time John got perhaps twenty regular business accounts who found his service a convenience and relied upon him, whenever they needed anything from business stationery and cards, to dis-play printing and brochures. He still gives a lot of work to the original printer who took a chance on him, but for work outside his field, such as color-process printing, John has now made connections with several other printers. He's active, happy in this new undertaking, and is making out very nicely in a brand new career that he invented when he was nearing seventy years of age. My brother John hung in there won-derfully, even when the going seemed to be hopeless. I'm grateful that we have the same genes.

3. *During the past month, have at least a couple of things arisen which at first blush struck you as being attractive, but which in the end you didn't do?* (*You*

probably felt they were either "too much trouble" or "not worth the bother.") Have you passed up such opportunities?

Yes_____ No_____

If you marked no, you are either a most remarkably outgoing person, or you are kidding yourself. At almost any age, the average individual would have to reply yes to this question, and the older we get, the more certain it is that this would be the answer. Yet it is exactly in our latter years that we should consciously exert ourselves to step out and savor even every semiattractive prospect that bobs up on our horizon. That's a fundamental aspect of hanging in there throughout a long life. No one can bury a body that keeps moving around!

Part Four

Yes, You Can!

Chapter Eleven

A Time for Thinking

I DON'T KNOW if Thomas Watson ever reaped any benefits for IBM when he instituted the policy of having
beautifully framed signs saying THINK in all the executive
offices. Perhaps he indeed did, but the general reaction about
this psychological ploy was ridicule and hearty merriment. I
suspect the whole thing benefited the humorous cartoonists
of the nation somewhat more than it did IBM.

Yet Mr. Watson wasn't really off the beam at all when he
hopefully dreamed up this particular piece of employee inspiration. Most of us in the Western world never find time
enough to slow down in our scurrying around and consciously put aside a daily time for thinking. This job has to be
done, that appointment has to be kept, an obligation must be
carried out, and even a pleasurable relaxation is squeezed in
between the tyranny of the clock and daily circumstances.
True, in the last few years, many people from our culture
have taken up Eastern ways of thought, ranging from Zen
and Yoga to transcendental meditation, and in many respects
I believe they may well have latched onto something very
helpful. Taking thought is the preliminary to everything else
one may do (or choose not to do), and while only a few may
decide to plunge wholeheartedly into Eastern ways, it's certain that all of us could benefit if we gave over some portion
of our time to contemplation. But since I am a complete

Westerner, with absolutely no background or training that would enable me to pose as even a bush-league guru, I'm going to address my simple ideas to an extremely simple suggestion: just take some time out to think.

Most of us spend our waking hours throughout our lives being "busy." We're busy preparing and eating meals, cleaning up and doing housework, getting to our jobs on time and carrying out our functions, seeing friends, telling off enemies, playing games and participating in sports, making love. If we do any sustained thinking at all, it's likely to be when we bed down for the night, and then it's likely to be thinking about the problems of the day. All that that sort of thinking produces are insomniacs.

Yet thought — pure thought with no more notion of where it may be heading and what its results may be than is involved in pure scientific research — is a marvelously constructive potential that we all possess. Even if we never consciously pause to say, Now I will think for a while, we do so intermittently. Usually it occurs only when we're faced with a problem, but what I call pure thinking can bob up in anyone's mind when he or she is alone for a few minutes. I am a shaving and showering pure thinker, my wife is apt to be a bus-riding pure thinker. Any occupation that doesn't require real concentration may open the doors of your mind to the unaccustomed practice of really using your mind.

But do you ever regularly put aside a portion of the day — no matter how brief — to say Now I'll just think for a while? No, you don't, because you're too "busy." And that is the way I've been too, all my adult life.

Up to now.

I have not yet retired and, with a couple of children still to put through college, and while continuing to enjoy my office work, I have no specific intention to do so for a while. But I have reached traditional retirement age and have been fortunate enough to be able to start easing off on the pressure aspects of the job I formerly did. That gives me some extra time for thinking, and now I spend anything from a very few minutes to quite some time each day simply trying to think constructively. I may concentrate on something to do with my office work, I may think about what I next intend to say in the book I'm writing. Or I may think about my wife

or one of my children, and come up with some fresh idea that would be rewarding or loving or just sheer fun. Concentrating and then popping up with what seems to you a gem of an idea is rewarding and fun in its very self. (But remember — it's pretty well negated if you then don't carry it out!) It can range from something as worldly as dreaming up an original, sure-fire sales promotion campaign for your product, to something as romantic as remembering that anemones are your wife's favorite flowers and bringing a bunch home. (But remember — unexpectedly — *not* just on her birthday.)

If, like me, you are still working but have a little more relaxed time than once you had, use some of it to *think!* Unless you are a really methodical type, you don't have to take a kitchen timer, set it to go off at a certain time, and then reset it for a specified Thinking Session. But when whatever you're doing eases off, try resisting turning on the television set to watch something you really have no interest in, and turn on your mind instead.

Maybe something will come of it almost every time, and maybe it won't, but sooner or later you're absolutely sure either to produce constructive, satisfying ideas by specific thinking or to pop up with equivalent ones through sheer serendipity. Even if those ideas don't work out or backfire, as one classic joke about Thomas Edison goes, there's a reward in simply having dreamed up what you thought might be a good idea.

Did you ever hear the Thomas Edison story? It seems he was having trouble for months inventing the incandescent light, but finally one evening, after brooding over what was wrong with the filament, he hit upon what he thought might be the solution. So he worked on it a few more hours through the night, fabricated the bulb, and tried it. Eureka!

It lit up brilliantly, and there was the world's first incandescent light, shining in all its glory!

So he rushed to the bedroom, shook his wife, and shouted "Wake up, darling, and come and see what I've done!" She opened her eyes, looked at him sleepily, and said, "Oh Thomas, turn off the light and come to bed."

That's a really spectacular put-down of an idea, but in the end Thomas Edison made out all right by thinking.

So in the period when you've been smart enough to become aware that your circumstances are changing, start practicing thinking in your spare time. Imaginative thinking leads to doing, and you will be preparing yourself well for the day that's coming, when you find yourself stranded on the beach. It's somewhat comparable to the way a relief baseball pitcher prepares himself for the catastrophe that seems likely to overwhelm his predecessor on the pitching mound. He rushes out to the bullpen and starts throwing hard, practice pitches to warm up. When he's finally called in to relieve, he's ready to go all out.

When and if you finally do retire completely, if there is one thing you will then have in abundance, it's time. Actually that is the basic problem for so many retirees, and seeing to it that it doesn't become a problem, but instead an opportunity, is what hanging in there is all about. Admittedly, unless you now plan to become a mystic or a philosopher, it will be in the *doing* that you will be a successful hanger-in-there, but the first step along the road is thinking about the doing, and from then on the doing inevitably has to be accompanied by more thinking.

But let's face the fact that you may feel you are not likely to be a self-starter in this type of thing, and that if you sat quietly for a period of time, simply concentrating upon trying to think, the only constructive thought that would cross your mind would be a desire to get up and do something. Don't be discouraged, for you have a great deal of company if you feel that way, and it's not because you're incapable of thinking. You merely have not ever been exposed much to a world of stimulating ideas, or it's been so long since you have been exposed that you're out of practice. Now you need a catalyst to spark your mind, and the answer could very well be for you to plunge into some adult education courses. The back-to-school boom for adults of all ages, and specifically for the middle-aged to the elderly, is a heartening phenomenon of our times. It has always been a notable way of life in some countries, particularly the Scandinavian ones, but it is only in recent years that it has truly been coming into its own in the United States. Here, even among those who loved and respected education, we have thought of school and college in tidy terms of age. One got through the grade school in eight years, high school took another four and college an additional four, and then one was approximately twenty-two years old and education was over. It was time for the serious business of life to commence, such as selling bonds.

After World War II, the flow of veterans who were substantially older than twenty-two into the colleges started to break the rigid concept of the proper age for schooling. At first this was regarded by the academics as anything from amusing to an actual threat to the existing scholarly standards, but today the idea of lifelong education has caught on, even in many of our most traditional and prestigious institutions.

Did you read the newspaper story last year about Harry Gersh? He is the second generation of his family to go to

Harvard — the first was his son. Mr. Gersh enrolled as a freshman at the age of sixty-three and, at last reports, was not only achieving grades well above the class average, but was having a marvelous time. He is quoted as saying that the only realistic problem he saw in his going through the university's four years of undergraduate study and earning his degree was money. "My son had it much easier," he said. "He had a rich father."

Well, I wouldn't maintain that every sixty-three-year-old is equipped to emulate Harry Gersh, but his determination and capabilities at his age set a noble example of what the elderly person can aspire to reach. Freshmen at Harvard are not eligible to play varsity football, and few sophomores make the team for that matter, but by the time Mr. Gersh's

junior year rolls around I'll be glancing at the sport pages now and then to see if, by any chance, Harry Gersh is a candidate for the T-formation quarterback spot.

On a more realistic plane, be assured that you don't have to have any previous connections to have many opportunities to go back to school or college. Write to your State Department of Education to find out what exists in your locality in the way of state colleges or universities, community colleges, or even local school systems that offer adult education courses. At a national level, there are several agencies in Washington, D.C., that offer information and advice to help you find what you're seeking. Among them are:

U.S. Office of Education, 400 Maryland Avenue S.W., Washington, D.C. 20202.

National Association for Public Continuing and Adult Education, 1201 Sixteenth Street N.W., Washington, D.C. 20036.

Adult Education Association of the United States, 810 Eighteenth Street N.W., Washington, D.C. 20006.

These agencies will send you helpful publications, as well as individual suggestions and advice, if you approach them. They can be the catalyst that will help you find the course that, in turn, can be your catalyst in waking up your mind again and giving you new material to think about.

The beautiful part of it is that you will truly have time to think. Each day there will be time that you can consciously put aside in which you'll do nothing except experiment with constructive thinking. You may amaze yourself with the ideas that will occur to you, with the fresh and unexpected slants about yourself and those important to you that will emerge, and with the actions that they will inspire.

Chapter Twelve

Hobbies in General

THE GREAT CANADIAN PHYSICIAN AND SCIENTIST Sir William Osler was an outstanding example of a man of varied interests and achievements that won him worldwide acclaim. He revolutionized medical teaching when he established his new medical school at Johns Hopkins University and wrote what is probably the most long-lived and popular textbook in the English language, *Principles and Practices of Medicine*. Osler led the most important and productive of lives throughout his career, and he is a prime example of hanging in there as well for, as he approached his sixtieth birthday, he crossed the Atlantic and took up a new post at Oxford, as Regius Professor of Medicine, where he continued to write and to collect classical medical texts. His will bequeathed his magnificent library of over 7500 items to McGill University and that is, along with its catalogue, the *Bibliotheca Osleriana*, perhaps the most impressive monument any physician has ever had.

Osler was much more than a magnificent physician. He was a man of many parts, universally loved as well as respected, and he was very conscious of the fact that all work and no play was likely to make William a dull boy. In late life he had the following to say:

No man is really happy or safe without a hobby, and it makes precious little difference what the outside interest may be —

botany, beetles or butterflies, roses, tulips or irises; fishing, mountaineering or antiquities — anything will do so long as he straddles a hobby and rides it hard.

It is possible that you may already have a hobby, or find one at this stage of your life, that in itself can actually fill all the requirements for your hanging in there. It may fill your waking hours with interest and pleasure, and it may even have enough commercial potential to earn money. That would be tremendously satisfying, and if you are fortunate enough to be able to pursue your hobby for the rest of your life with those sorts of rewards, your retirement years may well be the happiest of all.

Let's face the fact, however, that this will be true as a rare exception. A hobby is generally a very important sideline of a man or a woman's life, but no more than a sideline. A hobby usually is a way of pleasantly passing an hour or, at most, a very few hours of a day, and then one wearies of it. It is not a substitute for a style and way of life, but it may be the gateway toward your finding one. Also, whether or not it does, a hobby that simply fascinates or entertains you supplements enjoyable existence to an unmeasurable extent.

Sir William Osler made his remarks as part of a speech at a testimonial dinner in his honor, so the list he gave of possible outside interests is understandably brief. He was too much of a gentleman to entrap dinner guests past the point where the coffee grows cold, but had he chosen to elaborate on the myriad number of hobbies that people can undertake, hot coffee would have to be served again, for it would have been time for breakfast. Bookstores and libraries have scores of books devoted to the pursuit of one hobby or another, and there are also literally dozens of publications, one or more of which you may care to subscribe to once you've found an occupation or craft or study that intrigues you. But let's say that up to now you've never given the idea much thought, and haven't any notion of what the possibilities are. The best first thing you can do, in my opinion, is to get on the mailing list of U.S. Government publications. The Government Printing Office issues a great number of books and pamphlets on every imaginable topic, from the most serious of academic tomes to how-to-do-it volumes that almost invariably are as good, informative, and authoritative as any commercial book you could ever find. What is more, in relative terms, they are so inexpensive as to be fantastic book bargains. You will not have to write out a very big check to obtain quite a number of them, if several subjects intrigue you enough to wish to learn about them, and if in the end you discard all but the one you like best, your expenditure upon the others will be one of the cheapest pieces of investigation you'll ever come across.

Really. Do this. Write to the Superintendent of Documents, U.S. Government Printing Office, Washington, D.C. 20402, and ask for a free leaflet entitled "How to Keep in Touch with U.S. Government Publications." That will give you something like fifty subjects or areas of interest under each of which is a list of certain titles and their prices, and that will get you started. If you were to run the gamut of what the Government Printing Office has to offer in the way of informational books, booklets, and pamphlets you couldn't begin to make room for them, for there are something like 30,000 different titles on almost every imaginable topic and, besides being incredible bargains in these inflationary times, they are almost uniformly excellent publications, authoritative and well written. The range of subject matter that is available extends far beyond hobbies, and you may well find publications that are even more valuable to you on such topics as consumer information, pensions, insurance, conservation, recreational areas, homes, investments, health, Social Security, and Medicare. But we are thinking about hobbies right now, and there's almost surely a government publication that can help you get started, and give you sound advice, on just about every hobby man or woman has ever dreamed up.

Let's put aside those completely sedentary occupations and hobbies that may interest you intensely, and which always have been a source of pleasure to you. You don't need any advice about continuing to read books if you always have, or to listen to music, or to enjoy sports as a spectator. When you have much more time to spend as you please, you may well do even more of this sort of thing, and far from there being anything wrong about that, such pursuits offer a valuable and enjoyable change of pace from your fundamental way of life. But don't delude yourself that you can make a satisfying later career out of nothing but looking on. When you confine your days to watching or listening to what others are doing, and do nothing yourself with your mind or hands or body, you're just existing. Not living. Not really hanging in there, and continuing to be the person you know you once were and still are, if you'll rise to the challenge.

Here are examples of the sorts of activities and interests that possibly could intrigue and excite you. Not all of them, of course, but it's almost inconceivable that you won't find something in this listing that you feel you not only might like to do, but could do. But even if you don't, be of good heart. There are a zillion other activities that people engage in for fun or profit, which I simply didn't think about or chose to ignore. (Let's think of a couple offhand, just as examples: constructing crossword puzzles, exchanging chips for cash as the cashier of a gambling casino; doing something almost demented in order to win yourself a line in the *Guinness Book of World Records.*)

If you don't find an attractive hanging-in-there occupation among the suggestions that follow, you will if you write for that government publications catalogue. Not that it's the only good possibility to spark your imagination: places like your local Y's often offer fabulous and inexpensive courses that teach the techniques of a great many interests such as those we'll be discussing. Send for their catalogues, and those of museums, community colleges, and adult education schools as well. Many people will probably find, at least at the outset, that being part of a learning group is more exciting and more pleasant than trying to master something alone. Do a lot of reconnaissance and give a lot of consideration to what you think you'd want to take up, before you actually do it. It will help you pick the right thing and avoid disappointment, and it only costs a few postage stamps.

Chapter Thirteen

Hobbies in Particular

W HEN YOUR CATALOGUES start coming in, here are the sorts of things that you'll find either are taught in classes or for which how-to books are available. Just to show no favoritism, because I'd certainly like to do some of these things myself and equally would avoid others by as great a distance as I could put between myself and them (but I'm not *you*), they're listed alphabetically.

Accounting
(This *would* turn out to be the first alphabetically! In the classic words of Sam Goldwyn, "include me out" on this one. But you are not me, and perhaps accounting may be your special dish.)

There was a day when the creative people were the successes, and that was followed by the era of the brilliant salesmen. Today it's the C.P.A. types you find running businesses, so if the whole idea of depreciation allowances and tax shelters strikes you as the most fascinating pursuit to come along since Helen of Troy, this would be a splendid hanger-in-there occupation. Some accountants work full time, and some part time as free-lancers, and if it suits your temperament and talents, I doubt if you can do better.

Astronomy

Exploring the sky is fascinating, and a keen interest in astronomy could easily be an answer to what one might like to do. I think you had better not have money worries, however, if you choose this hobby, for it's doubtful that you can make anything out of it. And equipment, from simple binoculars to even a comparatively modest telescope, costs quite a lot. If the idea strikes your fancy, however, and you can afford to make it your hobby, you can build your own telescope with not too much difficulty at a substantial saving and get a lot of satisfaction in the process to boot.

Auctions

There are few attractions that have as much allure for people of all ages and circumstances as attending an auction sale, and this is true whether you're contemplating bidding and buying, or merely being a spectator to the action. There are city auctions and country auctions being held every day in just about every section of the country, and even in the unlikely event that you're not interested in trying to pick up even one bargain, the entertainment is free and invariably extremely enjoyable. I know a couple who started to attend auctions simply for fun, scanning the local newspapers for announcements of forthcoming auctions, and found them so enjoyable that they spent the better part of two or three days of every week at them, without trying to buy a thing. Gradually they began to appreciate the beauty of certain articles, the value of others, and felt sophisticated enough to start bidding for objects that appealed to them, and that they could afford. Today, a couple of years later, they run a successful antique shop and they have collaborated in the writing of a book about how to attend, enjoy, and buy at auctions.

Autographs

Collecting autographs is one of those hobbies that can run the complete gamut from doing so purely for one's own satisfaction and possible display, to making some money out of it. Believe it or not, autographs can often be picked up by luck, simply by writing and asking (although with celebrities you may merely get back a signature penned by an automatic signing device, which is easily discernable and is worthless), or through auction sales, dealers, and by trading with other collectors advertising in collectors' publications. It's a grown-up form of collecting and trading baseball cards and is equal fun.

Baking

Need I say more to the good ladies who have always been known for this talent, but only to their families and friends? Once the word is out in your community that you're in the business of making goodies for cash, and charge less for better cakes and cookies than the commercial bakery (which you can do, since you have no overhead), you may wonder how long this has been going on, and why you didn't do it long ago. Parenthetically, there's no reason except for outdated convention, that I should think of baking as a woman's hobby. Many men are wizards at it and enjoy it a lot, particularly the baking of bread.

Basketry

Here is another satisfying skill that fundamentally has been thought of as feminine, but for no particular reason. Such variations as basketry jewelry and fiber sculpture can supplement the construction of traditional baskets of various sizes, types, and shapes, and a great deal of creative artistry can be brought to it.

Birds

Bird watching has become so well recognized as a fascinating and rewarding study for those who fall in love with it, that it needs no more mention here than a reminder that as a hobby this is a possibility and that millions all over the world obviously enjoy it to the hilt.

Bookbinding

This is a craft course I took myself recently, restoring books that I cared for or valued. One learns to bind in full and half cloth, in leather, with gold print on the spines, or whatever. Even though supplies are not cheap, the cost is a small fraction of what rebinding the family Bible would stand you if you sent it to a professional firm and the satisfaction of doing it yourself is immense. Is it something out of which you could make any money? Some, I would think, if you get a local reputation for doing nice work, but pin money at best, I would guess. Essentially, one does it for oneself.

Calligraphy

This is another skill that is more likely to afford you great pleasure and elicit admiration than make you rich. However, if you become adept at italic handwriting (Chancery cursive), and Roman and Gothic lettering, you may well be able to offer your services for designing and executing award credentials, diplomas, signs, invitations, and the like. It is so unusual a skill that you haven't much competition, and the beautiful work of a calligrapher is highly valued. For example, my wife and I tend to avoid the more stuffy aspects of traditional etiquette so, when our elder daughter was about to be married a few years ago, we did not make a bee-line to Tiffany's for engraved invitations to the ceremony. Instead, we happened to know a splendid calligrapher, and she designed and executed a charming and beautiful invitation that the recipients will recall with pleasure long after they would have forgotten a traditional engraved wedding invitation.

Candlemaking

There are quite elaborate techniques that are taught, for candles can be much more than something you're glad you have when there's a power shortage. Gift shops display the most imaginative and lovely candles, many of them so stunning that it would take someone like Attila the Hun to think of ever burning one. Instruction involves such matters as clay and sand casting, torching, coloring, and inlay techniques. It's a long way from what you did in kindergarten.

Catering

Like baking, the person who always enjoyed making fairly elaborate goodies to go with the drinks can be a godsend for less talented or less ambitious neighbors, once the word gets around that she (or he) will supply you with canapés and hors d'oevres if you throw a small purse of gold at her (or him), over and above the costs. The caterer may indeed be asked to the parties as well.

Ceramics

This is so big and logical a field for anyone interested in crafts to try that I cannot even begin to detail the possibilities. The beauty of becoming a skilled ceramics performer is that what you produce is something people really may want, ranging from jewelry to ceramic bowls and vases. If you're good enough, you're in business. If you're not, at least you will have enough ash trays around the house.

Coins

A fascinating hobby, which can turn into a lucrative business once you learn it, and if you have a talent for it, but you do have to learn it first. It's nice that, while you're doing so, the equipment is minimal and inexpensive — a catalogue and a magnifying glass. Go easy for a while until you're sure you know what you're doing, but then with a little original capital, you can very possibly start a whole new career that will pay off. The literature about coins is very extensive and constantly being revised and updated, so you have to keep on your toes.

Collections

Of all hobbies, this has the greatest variety of choices. People have fun, and some make money, collecting absolutely everything from buttons to Rolls-Royces. This chapter has already touched upon collecting autographs and coins, and other popular pastimes like stamp collecting will be along soon. But the roster of what has been found to be diverting by assiduous collectors is staggering. Here are some of the more appealing that *Hobbies*, the magazine for collectors, has covered. (Certain collections strike me as positively insane, such as collecting barbed wire — which actually is listed — but if Sir William Osler could say that anything goes, I won't protest. To each his own, but barbed wire is not for me.)

On the other hand, I can see possibilities in many of these, and perhaps you can too.

Barber poles

Books (rare, first editions, autographed)

Bottles (really big possibilities here)

Buckles

Buttons (another large canvas, despite the invention of the zipper. And what about old political campaign buttons?)

Cartoons (comic ones are all right, but political ones probably will make a more important and interesting collection.)

Chessmen (fantastic possibilities, but likely to be expensive)

China (no end of possibilities)

Clocks

Comic books (do you know that an *Action #1*, starring Superman, recently brought $1800?)

Furniture (antique, dollhouse, miniature garden)

Glass

Guns (pistols and rifles, please. No howitzers or cannons)

Keys (we all collect these through the years for no reason except reluctance ever to toss them out. A planned collection might well be interesting, apart from the consideration that it could also be useful in case your hanging-in-there plan is to be a second-story burglar.)

Models (airplanes, automobiles, buses, ships, trains)

Phonograph records and tapes

Photographs

Posters (from presidential campaigns to entertainers)

Recipes (a practical suggestion that, at the least, can enhance living and, at the best, make a gourmet chef out of you)

Scrimshaw (articles of whalebone that have been engraved with all sorts of designs. John F. Kennedy was an ardent collector of scrimshaw. Possibly you would find it exciting to try your own hand at fabricating scrimshaw — in that case there's precedent that you could call yourself a "scrimshander," even though the basic dictionary definition terms that word simply a synonym for scrimshaw. So call yourself a scrimshander! It would be a lovely piece of gamesmanship in an arts and crafts conversation.)

Sheet music

Swords (various fencing types, ceremonial, hara-kari, etc.)
Theater programs
Wines (or, if that's too expensive, wine labels)

Offhand, I can't think of anything that comes after W except x-rays, and that would make a depressing collection. I don't recommend it. So let's move on to the next hobby.

Dogs

If you're a dog person (I refuse to call anyone a dog lover other than another dog), or a cat person for that matter, there is no doubt that the opportunity exists in almost any community to make anything from pin money to quite a lot of money. On the one hand, people go away for weekends or on vacation, and simply want a dog or cat boarded, or perhaps only tended in the home. Simple and pleasant if you are a dog or cat person, but you're not going to corner the wheat market on what you make out of *that*. On the other hand, suppose you know enough to breed pedigreed animals? Reason totters at what could come out of that.

Drawing and Sketching

An absolutely splendid hobby for all — even those who feel they "can't draw a straight line" (the fact is that straight lines don't exist in nature, and the inability to draw one may even give these people an advantage). Anyone can draw, admittedly more or less well. Those who do it less well may enjoy it just as much as those who excel, for the real joy of drawing and sketching lies in the stimulation of our awareness of things about us.

Enameling

If you didn't skip Chapter 2, you know about this. All I would add is that my wife's enamels sell whenever she cares to offer any, and our apartment is graced with the loveliest of things. There are several techniques one can learn: cloisonné, painting, plique à jour, champlevé, grisaille. Do some reading before you decide to take it up.

Fish

There are two completely different possibilities, as far as our finny friends are concerned. You can set up anything from the most simple and modest aquarium, to a veritable showplace that Flo Ziegfeld would have been proud of, but both of these will be for your own pleasure. If you'd like to combine pleasure with profit, follow the example of so many pier fishermen in thriving waters, who sell their catch daily to local restaurants. From lobster pots in Maine, to pompano in Florida, this pastime combines sport with business to a degree matched by few hobbies.

Flowers

Grow them for your own enjoyment and the beautification of your residence. And while you're at it, perhaps you can build up a small business selling off some of what you grow. Also, while you're at it, think of putting into a section of your garden the easier-to-grow vegetables which, apart from probably being fresher and better and cheaper than anything you're able to buy in the market, can also turn into a profitable venture for you if you have a green thumb.

Flute

Learning to play any musical instrument would get my vote as perhaps the most satisfying of all hobbies, and the flute was only selected by me because, unlike a pipe organ or even a harp, it's easy to carry from place to place in the subway. Besides, I like flute music, but then I also like the recorder (much easier if you're not that ambitious), the harmonica, the clarinet or oboe, all the stringed instruments, the brasses, and the piano. I must confess that I can live without cymbals.

Foreigners

Here's a volunteer hobby-job that is always welcome, and that can justifiably give you immense satisfaction if you're capable of doing a good job. Teach foreigners English. The best technique does not require the old academic approach of learning declensions and tenses, but simply conveys the useful words and phrases of the language by conversational English teaching methods. Anyone endowed with patience, understanding, and enthusiasm can do it — you don't require a Ph.D. or even a high school diploma.

Fossils

Few hobbies can so capture the imagination and life interest of an amateur as the study of fossils. Once a person digs up a trace of an animal or plant that existed anything from thousands to millions (or even billions) of years ago, he or she is hooked. The paleontology or geology department of a natural history museum will give you information, recommend or supply literature, and probably will be able to tell you about clubs of fossil enthusiasts who will welcome a newcomer to accompany them on field trips.

Gemology

This is another fascinating science. Museums and adult education courses teach everything from methods of identification to lapidary techniques.

Genealogy

I once knew a man who had a rather unusual name and who, quite by accident, met another man with the same family name. They talked and by comparing notes realized that they were distant relatives, which so sparked this man's curiosity in finding out more about his genealogy that it became a major interest that occupied his time for a long period. One name supplied led to another, and he instituted a voluminous correspondence with people here and abroad who might turn out to share his forebears. Not always satisfied with correspondence, he traveled and interviewed the ones who seemed most interesting and informative and then, when he had carried his research as far as he could, he sat down, drew up a family tree, and using that as a chronological working guide, actually wrote a book-length history of his family. Collaterally, he had been doing the same thing with his wife's family, and she had enthusiastically joined him in the research, so the final chapter was the linkage of the two lines with their marriage and the birth of their children.

The entire enterprise occupied the better part of two years with, of course, no commercial aim at all. It simply got to be an intriguing quest for the couple and, in the end, they took the manuscript to a vanity publisher (a publisher who gets paid to produce a book for an author, rather than the other way around) and had a small number of copies printed and bound. That was just for their own pleasure and that of the people whom they had interviewed and who had helped them in the preparation of the book. No one else in the world would give a hoot about the information it contains, but it is this family's proudest possession. Each child has his or her copy to own when establishing their own families in the future, and what a good and indeed productive and satisfying time this man and his wife had in carrying out the entire mission! So much so that they now offer their services to perform the same thing for other people, who haven't the time, energy, or ability to do it themselves. They realize that such assignments can't afford them the same personal excitement as they had unearthing their own antecedents, but these could possibly be equally or more interesting in other ways. (They themselves didn't have a single really fascinating forebear. No member of the nobility or even a western horse thief, poor devils.) Additionally, working for others they are being paid for their detective work, rather than footing the bills themselves.

I've gone into this example of the sort of hobby an imaginative person can get wrapped up in to a greater extent than it perhaps deserves, but it struck me as particularly unusual and original. Obviously, the man and his wife had to spend more money in what originally was a completely noncommercial project than most retirees could afford to spend. Between travel, and paying the vanity publisher, their costs must have been in the low thousands of dollars, but they had a marvelous time for a couple of years and, in the end, not only possessed something that meant more to them than a luxury purchase of comparable cost, but also had laid the groundwork for their own small business in the future.

Glass blowing

You need some inexpensive equipment for this one but, with just a little tutelage, you can almost immediately turn out *something* that will please you. A hideous swizzle stick with an almost round red head, for example (that was my first effort). After a while you can learn to turn out charming glass figures and objects, such as you see in Venice. (Or so I was told. A rather better swizzle stick was the best I could manage in my one-day experience at glass blowing.)

Hair styling

Suburban ladies with a flair for this have enticed customers away from the local hairdresser by offering as good or better a job, cheaper and under more pleasant home circumstances. Hair styling sounds more like a business than a hobby, but a person with such a talent, female or male, is an artist and enjoys the work in just the same way. It would be wise to check your local regulations on certification.

Insects

People with no previous experience, who think they might like to make a hobby of some natural history branch, turn easily to studies of birds and fishes, gardening and plants, with sea shells not too far behind. Fossils and rocks and minerals may well arouse curiosity too, but the first reaction to insects — and reptiles too — is likely to be sheer repulsion, accompanied by a new record for the standing backward long jump.

Reptiles can be fun, I'm told, but they are too special and too indigenous to particular regions to be likely to be your hobby. I'm sorry if you've been waiting all your life to turn to this page and learn something about reptiles but, if that's the case, at least you may find a few titles — perhaps *Lizards Make Lousy Lovers* — in the reptile category of reading *Books in Print.*

The study of insects can be an amazingly rewarding hobby. For one thing, you can find them anywhere in some form or other. There are over half a million kinds of insects in the world, and their bad reputation stems purely from the minuscule percentage of them that injure anyone or anything. As for the rest, they are around you in all their complexity and fascination, either merely to be observed or, perhaps, collected, living or as mounted specimens. There are entomological clubs you can join, and natural history museums often welcome help in this area from amateur volunteers.

Jewelry

This broad category can include everything from the study of gems, to the actual arts and crafts of lapidary work, enameling, silversmithing, and the fabrication of fine jewelry in settings. All of these things are offered in the Y's, community colleges, and adult education extension courses.

Additionally, there are the less ambitious practices of metalcraft, which, at best, can be pursued for sales and profit or, at worst, so that your husband can have more cufflinks, or your wife more earrings, than either of you can ever use up.

Knitting and Related Crafts

Need more be said than merely to mention knitting, which always has vied with baseball as the national sport. Today there are so many ramifications of skills akin to knitting that have also become wildly popular, such as crochet, needlepoint, spinning, weaving, macramé, quilting, and so forth, that the choice of areas is almost limitless.

Librarian

A wonderful job for anyone who thinks of it as a wonderful job, but to become a true professional librarian requires considerable training and expertise. Since we are discussing hobbies here, it may be helpful to realize that assistant librarians, working under a knowledgeable head librarian, can get much of the pleasure (if very little of the money) that the professional earns.

Mosaic tables

I once knew a man, of no particular manual dexterity but possessing a nice sense of design who, without any previous training at all, made a mosaic-tile table out of an ordinary glass-top coffee table that was as beautiful as a museum piece. It was so admired that he tried his hand at a few more, first for friends and then as a sideline business, and he made a lot of friends and quite a lot of money.

Mushroom hunting and collecting

This was the passionate hobby of an extremely eminent mathematician friend of mine. He would implore me to join him on certain mushroom hunting occasions, at the same time that I was imploring him to play tennis. To the eternal shame of both of us, neither ever succumbed to the other and, as a result, I know both of us missed out on something good. I can vouch that tennis is good, and since then I've met other extremely keen mycologists — (try *that* one on your next Scrabble opponent!) — whose general good sense I respect enough to believe in their enthusiasm. Maybe I'll try it some day, but not with eating in mind, unless I'm with someone who knows what he or she is doing.

Music

Just as a hobby, what about learning to sight-read musical notes? There's an entire world of pleasure that comparatively simple skill could open up for you, from following a score to learning how to play an instrument.

Oil Painting

The star attraction hobby of them all, as practiced by a whole string of notables including Winston Churchill and Dwight Eisenhower. It seems to me that it's almost irresistible to try your hand at oils at some time or the other, particularly when you know that frequently people with no previous experience do quite well at it right from the start. But don't overlook those companion arts — drawing and sketching, watercolor, acrylic, and so forth — which may appeal to you more than oil painting.

Photography

Taking pictures is a great and exciting hobby, and one that can often be turned to a profit. Individuals are often willing to commission and buy enlargements of a photograph you've taken of them and/or the members of their family, and if you get a local reputation you can very well be asked to take group pictures at weddings and other social occasions, graduations, sports events, and the like. If your photographs are good enough, you can sometimes even find a market for them in local newspapers. The real pleasure in photography, of course, is doing everything yourself, including the developing, printing, and enlarging. That sort of involvement in this hobby can really fill your spare hours in a most diverting and fascinating fashion.

Picture framing

I'll admit I never tried it, but this strikes me as an absolutely super hobby on all counts. It requires more than one skill in that you have to be something of a woodworker, a glazier, someone who got A's in school for neatness and accuracy, and a person with a sense of design, balance, and color. That isn't an overwhelming combination — many people possess these attributes, and the very variety of action and feeling that goes into picture framing would indicate that it's a lively and intriguing art to take up. I think that I may well do so one day and since, like you, I don't even know how to start, the first step will be to look over a couple of the dozen books on the subject that appear in *Books in Print.*

Apart from the satisfaction you may receive from conceiving and executing frames for your own favorite pictures and being able to sit back smugly over your beer or tea every evening admiring your handiwork, there is surely money to be saved or earned doing this well. Picture frames of any real substance and beauty are extremely expensive. If you want something framed handsomely, you may well have to pay much more for the frame than you ever spent on the subject. Much more. So at the very least, you can save a lot of money framing your own favorites.

As for earning money, I can only deduce that, if you've a talent for it, you can produce a commodity that has a definite market. Despite the fact that frames are so expensive, there are approximately one hundred and fifty picture frame *dealers* alone (not counting manufacturers or wholesalers) in the Manhattan yellow-pages telephone directory. If you can establish even a small, intimate reputation as a producer of custom-built mats and frames that can be purchased at substantially lower prices than the stores charge, you may find yourself making a very pleasant amount of money, even while doing it just as a hobby. If you turn out to be good enough, and like it enough, this is the sort of hobby that can well turn into a business after a while.

Puppetry

One thing leads to another in this field, and if you take a course in the construction and manipulation of hand and rod puppets, next you'll be designing stage sets and putting on marionette shows for children. Not that this is the summit of ambition: I have a dear friend named Frédéric O'Brady who was a master puppeteer in Europe. He made hand puppets out of Ping-Pong balls, and was flown over to this country twice to appear on "The Ed Sullivan Show." In passing, I must mention that this same Frédéric O'Brady is perhaps the most spectacularly effective hanger-in-there I know. Now well into his seventies and for that reason, and that reason alone, retired from the many distinguished things he did that paid him a regular salary, he is livelier and more active than ever. His talents and services are in constant demand, and no wonder, considering that he is a fine musician, a brilliant composer, a splendid actor and stage director, an author both of popular books and textbooks, a linguist and translator, and an inspired teacher. Please notice the verb tense is the present: *is*, not *was!*

Radio

Becoming a radio ham operator seems to me one of the most intriguing of all hobbies. If you wish to become one, you will have to train for it and pass examinations, but then you will join a happy and dedicated company of several hundred thousands of other hams, and you need never be lonely again. Hams talk to each other just for fun, either on a one-to-one basis or in a network. A new feeler from you in the form of a call to nowhere will always produce a reply. And, what is more, hams often are invaluable when disasters strike an area, providing communications when the normal ones have broken down. If you want to get started in this field, write to the American Radio Relay League in Newington, Connecticut 06111. They'll give you all necessary information.

Reading

If you've never been a reader, I'd guess it's pretty hard to think you'd start now — but you might try! If you are a reader, have you ever ventured past English and American literature? Wouldn't it be exciting to tackle the great Russian, French, German, and Japanese writers? Every foreign masterpiece has excellent translations into English — it could open a new world to you.

Stamps

Like coins, this is a hobby that you can start off easily and inexpensively. Perhaps you could always keep it at that level and find that it's enough to give you pleasure. There's no denying, however, that once bitten with the stamp or coin bug, ambition is likely to soar. When you find yourself about to mortgage your retirement house in sunny Florida in order to buy a famous stamp that has its center subject printed upside down, pause and remember that Spinoza called ambition a specie of madness.

Theater

Local amateur and some professional groups abound all over the country. Perhaps you're an actor, and perhaps you're a scenic designer, or just a stagehand. Finding out could be fun.

Travel

From the halls of Montezuma to the shores of Tripoli. Or to Atlantic City, for that matter. The travel bug is so extensive that all you need do is to look things over, count your cash and see what you can afford, and catch the next bus/train/ship/plane.

Volunteers

When a paying job isn't to be found, there is always a world of opportunity for a man or a woman who wants to work at something he or she would find interesting or that would be of public service.

With all due respect to the undoubtedly charming person you are, remember that you can be completely obnoxious and still, as an unpaid volunteer, be welcomed with open arms by those who need help. There are so many types of activities where volunteers form a vital function that a few minutes of thought on your part can produce an impressive list of possibilities. Here are a few, some of which may appeal to you or at least spur you to think of others: political campaign work; children's day care; hospitals; tutoring of students; neighborhood houses; assistants in museums; sports coaches and umpires; community gardening and beautification associations.

Weather forecasting

Although we have probably wondered at various times why the official weather reporter, who was still predicting fair skies when it was obviously raining, didn't bother to stick his head out of the window, the fact remains that meteorology is a justly respected science. You may have an impression that the weather forecasts are no better than about 50 percent correct, but you're wrong. They're a lot better than that, and if you study how to predict the weather and buy some not very expensive equipment, you will get a lot better than 50 percent accuracy too. Weather forecasting is a highly entertaining pursuit for a hobbyist, and what's more there aren't so many meteorologists around that, in a small community, you might not have a chance to be the local authority and become the Weather Man or Woman on the community radio station.

Weaving

From the simplest, tablet or card weaving, through more advanced pedal looms, to the elaborate Scandinavian, Kilim, and French tapestry techniques, there is a type of weaving for anyone who has a feel for color and composition.

Writing

Everyone has at least the equivalent of one book in him or her in personal experience. Have you any flair at putting it onto paper?

Although this has been a pretty long list, it could have been many times longer. One person's piece of nonsense can well be another person's devoted hobby, so practicing *anything* in spare time qualifies to be a hobby. Still, the goal of this book is not just to help you find a time-killer, which is the most some hobbies may turn out to be for a number of people, but rather to inspire you to create a fresh and satisfying active life for yourself. Some of the categories in my list offer a better chance for that than others, in my opinion, but the only opinion that's going to matter is your own. I might be irresistibly drawn to the idea of becoming a radio ham and repelled by the idea of studying accountancy, but if you have the opposite reaction you'll be making your fortune while I am simply chewing the fat with some stranger, one whom I am most unlikely ever to see, let alone get to know well. Let us each keep doing our own thing and take comfort from the fact that Sir William Osler would have said that we both were doing the right thing.

Chapter Fourteen

The Best Is Yet to Be

R OBERT BROWNING'S COMPLETE BODY OF POETRY
constitutes a monument of English literature, but some
of it is admittedly difficult and even obscure. The classic
example of this was his *Sordello,* the first line of which reads:
"Who will, may hear Sordello's story told" while the last line
is: "Who would has heard Sordello's story told." A learned
man once commented that those were the only two lines of
the poem that he understood at all, and that neither of them
was true!

Still much of Browning is simple, direct, and moving, and
two lines from his "Rabbi Ben Ezra" seem particularly so in
the context of this book:

> *Grow old along with me!*
> *The best is yet to be* . . .

That was written a quarter of a century after *Sordello,*
when Browning was in his fifties and still had another quarter of a century to live. It would be pleasant to imagine that
the lines were addressed direct to his beloved wife, Eliza-
beth Barrett, but she had died a couple of years before so we
must assume that they were merely the poet's poignant verse
about what might have been. That would have been characteristic of the man who delved so often into the relations
of men and women, and whose reputation for optimism

largely stemmed from his firm view that final defeat is un-imaginable.

Right on, Robert Browning! No matter what national statistics have to say about the decline of the marriage state and the increase of divorce, I doubt if anyone would contest the idea that, at least in your later years, you are likely to be wildly more happy if you share your life with a loved companion than if you spend your waking hours laying out interminable hands of solitaire.

But yes — I know. Fate handles us all in an infinite variety of ways, and many of us never encounter anyone whom we feel would be a compatible partner, or we do and it turns out to be a mistake, or we pick the solitary life by choice. And then there is the inevitability of death, which leaves one or the other person, up to then joined in perhaps a blissful union, suddenly and bleakly alone.

Yes — I know. And to try to discuss all these varying situations in one context is impossible, so let's look at them separately.

The happily married couple must have shared at least some common interests for years, and in one way this gives them a wide edge over all other hangers-in-there in later life. They can have each other's company, encouragement, and satisfactions. They may even undertake new enterprises or pastimes as a team, if they land upon something that suits both their temperaments and talents. Their sex lives, built up with each other over a long period, can (as studies by Masters and Johnson and Duke University show) extend into their eighties and nineties, with continued interest and capacity, for knowing that someone dear to you still cares for you in a physical sense can dispel the crippling aspects of sexuality that so often produce impotence in men, or loss of sensory feeling in women. Obviously, people's physical capacities change as they grow older, in sex as well as in everything else, but cessation of interest in sex and sexual performance almost invariably comes from psychological causes rather than physical inability.

A while back, the first piece in the *New Yorker's* justly famous section, "Talk of the Town," printed a letter that moved me a great deal. In it, the writer tells of a funeral he attended, and what it meant to him:

I had not been close to the woman whose funeral this was. Let's call her Mary Jones. She and her husband, Robert, had spent their summers in the community in which I, two generations younger, was growing up, and this meant that I had seen her often during my life but did not mean, as far as I could remember, that I had ever had a substantial conversation with her. She was, however, part of a privately held image; and it was in honor of this image that I was there, and with it that I contributed to the centripetal force in the room. Every summer for as far back as I could remember, I had watched Robert and Mary Jones walking down the beach to the water for a swim: she a tall, big-boned woman, clearly beautiful when young, a person with a languorous, faintly ironic style suggesting both character and humor; he a small man, distinguished (although not as glamorous as she), upright (in spirit and body), cheerfully earnest, energetic. A slightly comical couple because of their difference in size, they would walk at a leisurely pace, several feet apart, conversing. I never overheard much of what they said, but it was apparent that the conversation ranged from serious discussion to banter. Often it was punctuated with laughter; I remember the laughter most vividly. When they reached the water, they would wade in, still talking, losing their balance somewhat on the rocks underfoot, talk some more, and, finally, sink in and swim around a little — in a semi-upright position that allowed them to continue talking. Their enjoyment of each other was arresting — sharp as pepper, golden. I have seen other happy old couples, but this picture of the Joneses, renewed many times, came to represent to me an essence of human exchange — something indescribably moving and precious, which comes to fruition only toward the end of a lifelong marriage. Whatever that essence is, I find it dazzling. It has always struck me as one of the great possibilities life has to offer.

The happily married couple has much more to build upon in advancing years than simply continuing to be compatible in bed, desirable as that obviously may be. They can be partners in a host of things, significant ones or merely pleasurable ones, but they do face a real danger. Since they are two people, and not just one person, *both* of them must individually and jointly care about, and act upon the art of hanging in there. If, in seeking new priorities, they cannot light upon anything at all that is of common interest, each should seek out his or her own new enterprise and tackle it with passion. (Yes, "passion" is the word, even if it seems strong. To pursue a fresh interest in a feeble or dilettantish way is almost surely not going to be satisfying enough to make your hanging-in-there years what they should be, and can be. Ideally, you will get more deeply involved in what your new interest offers than you ever did in your work in the past, but even if that's not possible, you must at least find it engrossing some considerable portion of the time.)

The danger is that perhaps one person is indeed material from which a successful hanger-in-there will emerge, while the other feels incapable or frustrated or resentful, or all three. This means that the inspired one must infect the other with a comparable enthusiasm, not necessarily the same as his or her own, but with some work or pastime that can spark the other's enthusiasm. It doesn't have to be important or money-producing, but the other person has to become enthusiastically *involved* in something or other, or else he or she will become a drag upon the true striver to hang in there. Let neither one sulk over the other's new way of spending the hours, but instead find an intriguing pursuit of his or her own, and all will be well. They will go their separate ways for some time each day, but at the very least will meet over drinks before dinner on their porch or in their sunken conversation pit, eager to share their respective activities with each other. And each will succeed, because it's hard *not* to succeed at almost anything for which one has real enthusiasm. At least Charles Schwab, who certainly was a success, claimed that for a fact.

But let's presume that, for one reason or another, as detailed earlier in this chapter, you are alone. I have some comforting and, I hope, inspiring words for you.

Despite the fact that I attribute my own major joy in life to a happy marriage, there is a considerable body of deep thinkers today who put up an impressive case arguing that the important aspect of life is self-fulfillment and nothing much else. Adult education schools are over-registered in courses on expanding consciousness, awareness, transactional analysis, and coping through reality psychotherapy. Books on being your own best friend, self-realization, primal screams, *est*, and a host of other self-gratification life-styles boom high every month on the best seller lists. I would not presume to say which are good and which pure patent medicine, but my own viewpoint would be that such complete concentration throughout one's youth and middle age upon the self, with perhaps consequent disregard of rewards that mutuality has to offer, is a bleak and unfulfilling goal. Don't misunderstand Not being your own person, but relying upon and depending upon someone else is just as catastrophic a mistake at any stage of life. You have to stand on your own feet and be the individual you are capable of being. All I maintain is that two people, each solid individuals on their own, are likely to find a much more complete and satisfying life together, if they're compatible, than separately. Again I'd like to share with you a few lines from that same letter in the *New Yorker:*

We are coming to look upon life as a lone adventure, a great personal odyssey, and there is much in this view which is exhilarating and strengthening, but we seem to be carrying it to such an extreme that if each of us is an Odysseus, he is an Odysseus with no Telemachus to pursue him, with no Ithaca to long for, with no Penelope to return to — an Odysseus on a journey that has been rendered pointless by becoming limitless.

A Few Questions for You to Think About

1. *Do you have a sneaking feeling — or perhaps even a conviction — that today's tendencies to investigate ideas and philosophies that were foreign to the Western mind in your youth are nonsense?*

Yes_____ No_____

If you answered yes, I can understand the reaction, for I once had it myself. You and I were brought up in an era when the hard-working, down-to-earth precepts of Benjamin Franklin were golden rules. ("He that riseth late must trot all day" and "Lost time is never found again.") So you felt that things like meditation may have been okay for university philosophy professors and esthetes, but if you were going to emulate the rags-to-riches climb to success of the Horatio Alger, Jr., heroes, you'd better work hard, stick to brass tacks, and leave the meditation to Mahatma Gandhi.

But if you did, indeed, answer yes, I suggest that you might do very well for yourself if you opened your mind to what has been going on in the Western world in recent years, and how many people of intelligence and stature have found new values and inspiration in what used to be thought of as purely Eastern theologies. Tucked in among the wide range of such schools of thought are clearly a number that are nothing but fads or downright commercial exploitation, but to rule them all out for that reason, or because you're too set in your ideas to consider new ones, might indicate that you're poor material to be a successful hanger-in-there. Try thinking about that possible deficiency in yourself as a starter. It may lead to putting aside regular time to think and meditate about other things that will enrich your life.

If you answered no, you don't need a pep talk. But watch

out: it's true that a great deal of charlatanism is around too, trying to make converts of the credulous.

2. *Did you ever have a hobby that you once really enjoyed, but which you gave up for one reason or another?*

Yes____ No____

If yes, might you now want to rekindle your interest in it, and enlarge it, possibly to the point where you might even be able to make some money out of it?

If no, look over the vast number of possibilities that exist, and see if there isn't one which, even if you never practiced it before or had an enthusiasm for it, now perhaps sparks your imagination as something you'd like to try, and feel you could do well.

In either case, while the basic definition of a hobby is "an activity pursued for pleasure or relaxation," remember that a hobby can often become a business and a business can become a hobby. Those marriages are ideal ones when and if they take place, but the chances are a lot stronger that your hobby will be nothing more than your fun. So be it. Boredom and a waning of interest in life are greater enemies of a satisfying older age than anything else, and an engrossing hobby is the best antidote, whether it's remunerative or not.

3. *Do you believe that, whether you've been a gregarious person in the past or more of a solitary one, you now ought to cultivate as much self-reliance and self-fulfillment as you can?*

Yes____ No____

I won't give you a choice of yes or no on this question, because there's only one answer — yes. It really doesn't matter what your circumstances are going to be from now on. The answer is yes.

Take the person who is not going to be forced into retirement, but continues to work at the old job. That sounds as if everything is likely to go along in the same old comfortable pattern, but not only it ain't necessarily so, but it's not even likely to be so. Attitudes toward you will inevitably change at your place of work. You may continue to do a good job and be respected for it, but as your associates, and particularly those running the show, turn out to be of the next generation, the best you're likely to get from them is polite respect. You are not likely to socialize too often with them, as you once did with your contemporaries, and you may well find yourself uncomfortable in a new ambiance. So, even if things don't change at home, they are pretty sure to at work, and finding your own satisfactions there will become more significant to your happiness than it may have been in the past, when you were probably more wound up and involved in a team effort.

Suppose you are going to retire, whether by choice or by mandatory decree, and you're really not at all sad about it because you're very happily married to someone at home, and now feel that you'll have more time for each other. That's an enviable situation, and you have a great head start toward hanging in there with full flags flying all the way. But even in such a situation, there is a possible worm in the apple. For years you each spent a great portion of your waking hours being involved in activities that interested you and that you did separately. You may find that there are too many hours in the day and too many days to fill, with little on each of your minds except loving companionship. Wonderful as that may be, it alone is not enough. If you are partners in a business, or enthusiastically share a hobby, all is well, but that won't be true of most couples. So now, just as before, some major portion of each of your lives needs to be created in which each person does his or her own thing. This is what self-reliance and self-fulfillment are all about. The joys of sharing will come in appreciation and discussion of the other's interests, but meanwhile both of you will be doing something that engages your separate interests and fills the days with gratification, and neither of you will be going crazy trying to mold complete happiness out of no material other than sharing a love nest. The only people for whom that concept really worked were the lyric writers of popular songs in the 1920s.

Finally, if you've been a loner up to now, you probably don't need to think about your answer to the question. Certainly, you feel, you will cultivate self-reliance and self-fulfillment: you always have. That is undoubtedly true, but even you may need some re-evaluation of your priorities in this respect, for the world changes and if people are to move along in a new world fruitfully, they must change too. So don't settle for all your old ideas and habits, just because they served you well enough for years. Cling to those that still seem attractive, but open up your mind to anything that comes along, or that you read about in today's paper, that strikes you as a stimulating notion, or an intriguing pursuit. Age is no barrier to the undertaking of many things that are introduced by the enthusiasm or dedication of young people, since most of them don't depend at all upon physical ability or adroitness, but much more upon willingness to experiment with new ideas. Your limbs may stiffen, but don't allow your mind to do the same.

That is really the way to stay young, and staying young in this respect is really the way to hang in there.

Call me up in a few years and let me know how you make out. The energy and discipline that I myself had to summon in embarking upon a second career of writing, and the pleasures and rewards it is now giving me, make me optimistic about myself, and I am optimistic about you too.